The
REALLY USEFUL BOOK OF SECONDARY SCIENCE EXPERIMENTS

How can a potato be a battery?
How quickly will a shark find you?
What food should you take with you when climbing a mountain?

The Really Useful Book of Secondary Science Experiments presents 101 exciting, 'real-world' science experiments that can be confidently carried out by any KS3 science teacher in a secondary school classroom. It offers a mix of classic experiments together with fresh ideas for investigations designed to engage students, help them see the relevance of science in their own lives and develop a passion for carrying out practical investigations.

Covering biology, chemistry and physics topics, each investigation is structured as a problem-solving activity, asking engaging questions such as, 'How can fingerprints help solve a crime?', or 'Can we build our own volcano?' Background science knowledge is given for each experiment, together with learning objectives, a list of materials needed, safety and technical considerations, detailed method, ideas for data collection, advice on how to adapt the investigations for different groups of students, useful questions to ask the students and suggestions for homework.

Additionally, there are 10 ideas for science-based projects that can be carried out over a longer period of time, utilising skills and knowledge that students will develop as they carry out the different science investigations in the book.

The Really Useful Book of Secondary Science Experiments will be an essential source of support and inspiration for all those teaching in the secondary school classroom, running science clubs and for parents looking to challenge and excite their children at home.

Tracy-ann Aston is Lecturer in Education and Teacher Training, specialising in Science Education and Primary Teacher Training at the University of Bedfordshire, UK.

The Really Useful Series

The Really Useful Book of Science Experiments: 100 Easy Ideas for Primary School Teachers
Tracy-ann Aston

The Really Useful Maths Book: A Guide to Interactive Teaching,
2nd edition
Tony Brown and Henry Liebling

The Really Useful Literacy Book: Being Creative with Literacy
in the Primary Classroom,
3rd edition
Tony Martin, Chira Lovat and Glynis Purnell

The Really Useful ICT Book
Jill Jesson and Graham Peacock

The Really Useful Physical Education Book
Edited by Gary Stidder and Sid Hayes

The Really Useful Book of ICT in the Early Years
Harriet Price

The Really Useful Creativity Book
Dominic Wyse and Pam Dowson

The Really Useful Science Book: A Framework of Knowledge for
Primary Teachers,
3rd edition
Steve Farrow

The REALLY USEFUL BOOK OF SECONDARY SCIENCE EXPERIMENTS

101 Essential Activities to Support Teaching and Learning

Tracy-ann Aston

Routledge
Taylor & Francis Group
LONDON AND NEW YORK

Visit eResources: https://www.routledge.com/9781138192102

First published 2018
by Routledge
2 Park Square, Milton Park, Abingdon, Oxon OX14 4RN

and by Routledge
711 Third Avenue, New York, NY 10017

Routledge is an imprint of the Taylor & Francis Group, an informa business

© 2018 Tracy-ann Aston

The right of Tracy-ann Aston to be identified as author of this work has been asserted by him/her in accordance with sections 77 and 78 of the Copyright, Designs and Patents Act 1988.

All rights reserved. No part of this book may be reprinted or reproduced or utilised in any form or by any electronic, mechanical, or other means, now known or hereafter invented, including photocopying and recording, or in any information storage or retrieval system, without permission in writing from the publishers.

Trademark notice: Product or corporate names may be trademarks or registered trademarks, and are used only for identification and explanation without intent to infringe.

British Library Cataloguing in Publication Data
A catalogue record for this book is available from the British Library

Library of Congress Cataloging in Publication Data
Names: Aston, Tracy-Ann.
Title: The really useful book of secondary science experiments : 100 essential activities to support teaching and learning / Tracy-Ann Aston.
Description: Abingdon, Oxon ; New York, NY : Routledge, [2017]
Identifiers: LCCN 2016058235| ISBN 9781138192096 (hardback) | ISBN 9781138192102 (pbk.) | ISBN 9781315640082 (ebook)
Subjects: LCSH: Science—Experiments. | Science—Study and teaching (Secondary)—Activity programs.
Classification: LCC Q182.3 .A78 2017 | DDC 507.8—dc23
LC record available at https://lccn.loc.gov/2016058235

ISBN: 978-1-138-19209-6 (hbk)
ISBN: 978-1-138-19210-2 (pbk)
ISBN: 978-1-315-64008-2 (ebk)

Typeset in Palatino and Gill Sans
by Florence Production Ltd, Stoodleigh, Devon, UK

Printed and bound by CPI Group (UK) Ltd, Croydon, CR0 4YY

Contents

Introduction ix
How to use this book x

1	**Observation:** Are probiotic yogurts worth the extra money?	2
2	**Observation:** How similar are animal and plant DNA?	4
3	**Observation:** What do the inside of lungs look like?	6
4	**Observation:** Are all fats the same?	8
5	**Observation:** How do plants exchange gases?	10
6	**Observation:** How do apples decay?	12
7	**Fair testing:** Is salt a good preserver of food?	14
8	**Fair testing:** How can plants use wind to reproduce?	16
9	**Fair testing:** Are there enzymes in our liver?	18
10	**Fair testing:** What is the best food to take with you when climbing a mountain?	20
11	**Fair testing:** Which is the most dangerous sea to swim in if you are bleeding?	22
12	**Fair testing:** How quickly will our muscles tire?	24
13	**Fair testing:** Can we speed up the rate of photosynthesis?	26
14	**Pattern seeking:** Where do daisies grow?	28
15	**Pattern seeking:** Do taller people have larger hands?	30
16	**Pattern seeking:** Do insects prefer to live in the light or the dark?	32
17	**Pattern seeking:** Can long legs jump further?	34
18	**Pattern seeking:** Do our hearts beat faster when we work harder?	36
19	**Pattern seeking:** Are hand-dryers more hygienic than paper towels?	38
20	**Classification and identification:** Can you identify animal and plant cells just by looking at them?	40
21	**Classification and identification:** Can we classify leaves?	42
22	**Classification and identification:** What are the best fruits and vegetables to eat when you have a cold?	44
23	**Classification and identification:** How can fingerprints solve a crime?	46
24	**Classification and identification:** Which plants are growing near our school?	48
25	**Classification and identification:** What's in our food?	50
26	**Modelling:** Can we build a digestive system?	52
27	**Modelling:** Can we build a DNA separating chamber?	54
28	**Modelling:** Can we build a model of DNA?	57
29	**Modelling:** Can we ferment our own ginger beer?	59
30	**Modelling:** Can we build a bug hotel?	61
31	**Modelling:** Can we design and make a stethoscope?	63

32	**Observation:** Can a solid turn into a gas?	65
33	**Observation:** Where should we dig for oil?	67
34	**Observation:** What colour are M&Ms?	69
35	**Observation:** What is the best material for a campfire?	71
36	**Observation:** How can we make colourful flames?	73
37	**Observation:** What is special about the melting and freezing point of a substance?	75
38	**Fair testing:** Which is the best washing powder?	77
39	**Fair testing:** Can we prevent rusting?	79
40	**Fair testing:** Which antacid is the most effective?	81
41	**Fair testing:** Which is the best brand of disposable nappies?	84
42	**Fair testing:** How does temperature affect the rate of a reaction?	86
43	**Fair testing:** How quickly will a puddle evaporate on a hot day?	88
44	**Pattern seeking:** How quickly will a battery run down?	90
45	**Pattern seeking:** What is the hardest liquid to swim through?	92
46	**Pattern seeking:** Will aquatic plants grow in acidic water?	94
47	**Pattern seeking:** Do all oxides have the same pH?	96
48	**Pattern seeking:** Which element in group 2 of the periodic table is the most reactive?	98
49	**Pattern seeking:** Which element in group 7 of the periodic table is the most reactive?	100
50	**Classification and identification:** Are all changes reversible?	102
51	**Classification and identification:** What is the best soil for growing plants?	104
52	**Classification and identification:** How can we identify colourless gases?	106
53	**Classification and identification:** How can polymers be identified?	108
54	**Classification and identification:** Do chemical reactions always give off heat?	110
55	**Classification and Identification:** Does everything dissolve in water?	113
56	**Modelling:** Can we make our own fizzing bath bombs?	115
57	**Modelling:** Can we make popping fruit juice balls?	117
58	**Modelling:** Can we grow a crystal garden?	119
59	**Modelling:** Can we build our own volcano?	121
60	**Modelling:** How can cabbage be an indicator?	123
61	**Modelling:** Can we make a bouncing custard ball?	125
62	**Observation:** How many colours are there in light?	127
63	**Observation:** How does pressure vary in a water column?	129
64	**Observation:** What do waves look like?	131
65	**Observation:** Which objects will give you a static shock?	133
66	**Observation:** How do gases move?	135
67	**Observation:** How much 'stuff' do we make in a reaction?	137
68	**Fair testing:** How can we change the brightness of a bulb?	139
69	**Fair testing:** Why do moon craters vary in size?	141

70	**Fair testing:** What are the most dangerous weather conditions to drive in?	143
71	**Fair testing:** How can we increase the resistance in a circuit?	145
72	**Fair testing:** How can blood spatter solve a crime?	147
73	**Fair testing:** Can we stop radio waves?	149
74	**Pattern seeking:** How can you make a swing go faster?	151
75	**Pattern seeking:** Can you break a spring?	153
76	**Pattern seeking:** How can we make a magnet stronger?	155
77	**Pattern seeking:** How does light enter and leave a mirror?	157
78	**Pattern seeking:** How can we change the speed of light?	159
79	**Pattern seeking:** What happens to waves in shallow water?	161
80	**Classification and identification:** Which materials are best for keeping something warm?	163
81	**Classification and identification:** Which materials are best for building an electric circuit?	165
82	**Classification and identification:** Can we identify different types of radiation?	167
83	**Classification and identification:** Can we classify all materials as solids, liquids or gases?	169
84	**Classification and identification:** What is the densest liquid?	171
85	**Classification and identification:** Where is the energy going?	173
86	**Modelling:** Can we cook food using the sun?	175
87	**Modelling:** Can we make our own camera?	177
88	**Modelling:** How can a potato be a battery?	179
89	**Modelling:** Can we build a catapult?	181
90	**Modelling:** Can we design and make a musical instrument?	183
91	**Modelling:** Can we make a crash helmet?	185
92	**Project 1** Healthy teeth	187
93	**Project 2** Desert island survival	188
94	**Project 3** Environmental survey	190
95	**Project 4** Set design	192
96	**Project 5** Olympic science	194
97	**Project 6** Chocolate lab	196
98	**Project 7** Scene of crime investigation	198
99	**Project 8** Fairground games	200
100	**Project 9** Aeroplane design	202
101	**Project 10** What's the weather like?	203

Index 205

Introduction

ABOUT THIS BOOK

This book presents 101 science experiments based on the Key Stage 3 National Curriculum for science. The experiments are presented as problem-solving activities for the students to solve, helping them to see the relevance of science in their own lives. There is a mixture of classic science experiments along with new experiments that teachers may not have tried with their students before. I hope that both teachers and students will be inspired by the investigations and will develop a passion for carrying out practical science investigations.

WHY PRACTICAL SCIENCE INVESTIGATIONS ARE SO IMPORTANT WHEN TEACHING SCIENCE

We live in a world that is increasingly being dominated by scientific ideas and inventions. From the latest smart phones to global warming, students will need to have the knowledge and skills to navigate the science they encounter in their everyday lives. Unfortunately, the number of students studying STEM subjects (science, technology, engineering and mathematics) at university is declining, leading to a shortage of future scientists that we will desperately need. Students can often be 'turned-off' science by the image they have of what a scientist is and what they do (Silver and Rushton, 2008). They may have the perception that science is dull, repetitive and only carried out in a dusty laboratory. The truth, however, is very different. Scientists come from all walks of life and work in an incredibly diverse range of fields including pharmacists developing the latest drugs, marine biologists exploring the deepest oceans and astrophysicists designing new and better telescopes. The experiments in this book allow students to work together collaboratively, discovering new scientific ideas and principles for themselves in meaningful and relevant contexts.

TYPES OF SCIENTIFIC EXPERIMENTS

The experiments in this book are broken down into five different categories; observations, fair-testing, pattern-seeking, classification and identification and modelling. A description of the different types of investigation can be found below. By carrying out different types of science investigation students are able to develop a wide range of transferable skills and it also helps them to realise that not all science experiments have to be 'fair tests'.

- Observations: Carry out detailed observations of objects or phenomena
- Fair-testing: Carry out an investigation where one variable is altered whilst all other variables are kept constant
- Pattern seeking: Exploring relationships that may exist between objects or phenomena
- Classification and identification: Using properties of objects, materials or phenomena in order to classify or identify them
- Modelling: Design and make a model based on a scientific principle

There are also 10 ideas for science-based projects that can be carried out over a longer period of time, for example a week. The project ideas utilise skills and knowledge that the students will develop as they carry out the different science investigations in the book.

BIBLIOGRAPHY

Department for Education (DfE). (2013) National Curriculum in England: science programmes of study. London.

Silver, A. and Rushton, B. (2008) Primary-school children's attitudes towards science, engineering and technology and their images of scientists and engineers. *International Journal of Primary, Elementary and Early Years Education*, **36**, (1) 51–67.

How to use this book

This book presents 101 science experiments that are suitable for Key Stage 3 students.

This book is based on the (2014) National Curriculum for science but is not limited to the statutory programme of study. These experiments could be carried out in the secondary school classroom as part of the science teaching but could also be utilised in science clubs or by parents looking to challenge and excite their children at home. The experiments are divided into three sections: biology, chemistry, physics and projects. The experiments in the book are broken down into the following sections.

- Learning objective: The main teaching objective for the experiment.
- Introduction: A brief overview of the science experiment.
- Useful prior work: What the students should already know before completing the experiment.
- Background science: A brief overview of the science behind the experiment. This is intended for the teacher's benefit and is not necessarily indicative of what the students would need to know.
- National Curriculum links: Ideas of where the experiment fits into the Key Stage 3 National Curriculum for science.
- Materials: A list of the materials required for the experiment. Ideas for possible substitutions are included.
- Safety and technical notes: An overview of the safety and technical considerations of the experiment.
- Method: The method needed for the students to carry out the experiment including any preparatory work by the teacher.
- Data collection ideas: Ideas for how the results from the experiment can be collected and/or presented.
- Differentiation: Ideas for how the experiment could be made more or less challenging for different groups of students.
- Useful questions to ask the students: Some suggestions for questions that you could ask the students during and after the experiment.
- Homework: Ideas for homework activities based on the experiment.

All tables are available to download from the eResources site at https://www.routledge.com/9781138192096

EXPERIMENTS 1–101

EXPERIMENT 1

Observation:
Are probiotic yogurts worth the extra money?

LEARNING OBJECTIVES:
Use a microscope to identify the types and quantities of bacteria present in probiotic yogurts and plain yogurt.

INTRODUCTION:
The students prepare slides of different types of yogurt and examine them under the microscope to see if there is a difference between the quantity and strains of bacteria present.

USEFUL PRIOR WORK:
The students should know how to use a microscope and how to prepare a microscope slide.

BACKGROUND SCIENCE:
Yogurt is made by fermenting milk using bacteria. The bacteria feed on the sugar (lactose) present in the milk and produce lactic acid as a waste product. This acid is what gives yogurt its characteristic sharp taste. Probiotic yogurts are a specific type of yogurt that contain live active cultures of bacteria. These cultures have typically been added to the yogurt for their potential health benefits. The most common bacteria found in probiotic yogurts are *Lactobacillus bulgaricus* and *Streptococcus thermophilus.* These bacteria are thought to be beneficial to the human digestive system. This is because the digestive system contains bacteria that help to aid digestion, therefore by building up these colonies of 'good' bacteria it reduces the chance of harmful bacteria being able to establish themselves in the digestive system. All yogurts contain 'good' bacteria but probiotic yogurts are marketed as containing more of these 'good bacteria' than regular yogurts and subsequently are typically priced higher than regular yogurts.

NATIONAL CURRICULUM LINKS:

Cells and organisation
- cells as the fundamental unit of living organisms, including how to observe, interpret and record cell structure using a light microscope
- the structural adaptations of some unicellular organisms.

Nutrition and digestion
- the importance of bacteria in the human digestive system.

MATERIALS NEEDED:
Microscopes, slides, coverslips, swabs, dropper, water, plain yogurt – three different varieties, probiotic yogurt – three different varieties.

SAFETY AND TECHNICAL NOTES:

- You may want to use yogurts from a range of price points so the students can compare, for example, expensive plain yogurt with cheaper probiotic yogurt.

- Emphasise the importance of having a thin layer of yogurt on the slide so the bacteria will be more visible under the microscope.
- Remind the students not to consume any of the yogurt.
- Be aware of any allergies.

METHOD:

To be done in advance by the teacher

Identify the different strains of bacteria present in the yogurts that you will be using for the experiment. They will usually be found on the label or the ingredients list of the yogurt. Prepare a handout or slide that shows the shapes of the different bacteria and their names for the students to use in their identifications. Include some bacteria that are not present in the yogurts.

STUDENTS:

1. Choose the first yogurt you will be testing.
2. Use a swab to add a small amount of the yogurt to a microscope slide. Use the swab to spread the yogurt into a thin layer on the microscope slide.
3. Use the dropper to add one drop of water onto the layer of yogurt.
4. Add a coverslip to the microscope slide so that the layer of yogurt is covered.
5. Place the slide under the microscope and use the lowest power magnification to find a section of yogurt with bacteria present.
6. When you have located the bacteria, use a higher power magnification to examine the bacteria.
7. Draw what you can see and try to count how many individual bacteria are present.
8. Repeat the investigation for the other yogurts.
9. When you have examined all the yogurts try to identify which types of bacteria are present in the different yogurts using the handout you have been given.

DATA COLLECTION IDEAS:

Students can draw what they observe under the microscope and count the number of bacteria present. They can also identify the type of bacteria present in each yogurt.

DIFFERENTIATION:

- **Decrease the challenge:** Students could perform a simple streak test on an agar plate for each yogurt and grow the bacteria. They could then compare which yogurt produced the most bacteria.
- **Increase the challenge:** Students could perform a more accurate count of the number of bacteria present by using a counting chamber slide if this is available.

USEFUL QUESTIONS TO ASK THE STUDENTS:

1. Which yogurt do you think is the best one for your digestive system? Why do you think this?
2. Do you think probiotic yogurts are worth the extra cost? Why do you think this?
3. Was this the most accurate way of determining the quantity and types of bacteria present? How could we improve the investigation?

HOMEWORK:

The students can prepare an advertising poster for a probiotic yogurt including details of the bacteria present and why it is good for your digestive system.

EXPERIMENT 2

Observation: How similar are animal and plant DNA?

LEARNING OBJECTIVES:
Prepare a DNA extraction solution and use the solution to extract DNA from a plant cell and an animal cell.

INTRODUCTION:
The students prepare a DNA extraction solution using washing-up liquid, salt and alcohol. They then extract DNA from strawberries and liver and observe the extracted DNA.

USEFUL PRIOR WORK:
The students should know what DNA is and where it is found in a cell.

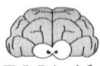

BACKGROUND SCIENCE:
DNA (deoxyribonucleic acid) is the genetic material found in all living organisms. The nucleus of every cell of a living organism contains the full complement of DNA for the organism. The DNA acts as a code for the organism, specifically coding for the formation of proteins. DNA is made up of smaller sub-units called genes. Each gene of an organism codes for one specific characteristic, for example blood group. DNA is shaped into a double helix (two strands wrapped around each other giving the appearance of a twisted ladder). DNA cannot be seen with the naked eye but can be observed under a microscope. To do this it must first be extracted from a cell. Strawberries work well for this as they have a large number of chromosomes. The DNA is extracted using an extraction solution. The washing-up liquid breaks down the cell membranes, releasing the DNA, and the salt breaks the bonds holding the two strands of DNA together. Alcohol is used as DNA is insoluble in alcohol. The DNA extracted from animal cells will typically be more defined than DNA extracted from plant cells as animal cells lack a cell wall (found in plant cells), which makes the DNA easier to extract.

NATIONAL CURRICULUM LINKS:

Cells and organisation
- cells as the fundamental unit of living organisms, including how to observe, interpret and record cell structure using a light microscope
- the functions of the cell wall, cell membrane, cytoplasm, nucleus, vacuole, mitochondria and chloroplasts

Genetics and evolution
- heredity as the process by which genetic information is transmitted from one generation to the next.

MATERIALS NEEDED:
Strawberries, lamb's liver, isopropyl alcohol, washing-up liquid, salt, ziplock bags, sieves, water, measuring cylinders, beakers, tweezers, pipettes, measuring spoons, stirring rods, black cardboard or paper, magnifying lenses, blender.

⚠ SAFETY AND TECHNICAL NOTES:

- Fresh or defrosted frozen strawberries can be used for this investigation.
- Make sure the alcohol is kept cold, ideally in a freezer, until it is needed.
- This experiment will work equally well using kiwi fruits instead of strawberries.
- Use lambs' liver to reduce religious issues when conducting this investigation.
- Some students may object to handling liver so an alternative activity should be available.
- The students should wash their hands after the investigation.
- Be aware of any allergies.
- Remind the students not to consume any of the fruit.

METHOD:

To be done in advance by the teacher
Chill the alcohol in a fridge or freezer (see safety and technical notes). Use a blender to purée the liver.

STUDENTS:

1. Add 90ml of water and 10ml of washing-up liquid into a clean beaker.
2. Add a 1/4 teaspoon of salt to the beaker. Stir the contents of the beaker.
3. Put one strawberry into a ziplock bag and pour the contents of the beaker into the bag. Close the bag and squeeze the strawberry using your hands. Try to make the contents as smooth as possible.
4. Pour the contents of the ziplock bag through a sieve into a new beaker.
5. Add 5ml of isopropyl alcohol to the solution in the beaker. Do not stir or shake the beaker.
6. Observe the surface of the liquid in the beaker. You should be able to see white strands on the surface. This is the DNA you have extracted.
7. Use tweezers to carefully remove the DNA. Place the DNA onto the black paper.
8. Use the magnifying lens to observe the DNA.
9. Repeat the investigation using a tablespoon full of the pureed liver instead of the strawberry.

✎ DATA COLLECTION IDEAS:
The students can take photographs of the different parts of the extraction process and the resulting DNA.

DIFFERENTIATION:
- **Decrease the challenge:** The students can have the DNA extraction solution prepared in advance for them.
- **Increase the challenge:** The students can extract DNA from different fruits and compare the results.

USEFUL QUESTIONS TO ASK THE STUDENTS:
1. What observations did you make of the DNA? Were you surprised by your results?
2. Where are there differences between the animal and plant DNA? Why do you think this was?
3. Why is it useful for us to be able to extract DNA from organisms?

HOMEWORK:
The students can research the work of James Watson, Francis Crick, Maurice Wilkins and Rosalind Franklin and decide who they think should be credited with discovering the structure of DNA.

EXPERIMENT 3

Observation: What do the inside of lungs look like?

LEARNING OBJECTIVES:
Perform a dissection of a sheep lung and identify the main parts of the lung and breathing system.

INTRODUCTION:
The students dissect a sheep lung or pluck using scalpels and scissors in order to identify the main parts of the breathing system.

USEFUL PRIOR WORK:
The students should know the role of the lungs in humans and the main parts of the breathing system.

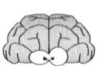

BACKGROUND SCIENCE:
The lungs form part of the respiratory system. They are large, spongy organs and are the site of gas exchange (humans need to take in oxygen and expel carbon dioxide). Air is inhaled through the mouth and nose and travels down the trachea (windpipe), which divides into two smaller tubes called bronchi. The bronchi then further divide into smaller tubes called bronchioles. At the end of the bronchioles are microscopic air-sacs called alveoli. The alveoli are where gas exchange takes place. The alveoli are surrounded by blood vessels that allow oxygen to diffuse from the lungs into the blood and for carbon dioxide to diffuse from the blood into the lungs. Healthy lungs should be pink and have a springy, sponge like texture. Diseased lungs, particularly those from people who smoke, will be darker or even black in places and will have a stiffer texture.

NATIONAL CURRICULUM LINKS:

Gas exchange systems
- the structure and functions of the gas exchange system in humans, including adaptations to function
- the impact of exercise, asthma and smoking on the human gas exchange system.

MATERIALS NEEDED:
Lungs or pluck (heart and lungs together), scalpel, dissection scissors, beakers, trays or white tiles, magnifying lenses, rubber tubing and foot pump (optional).

SAFETY AND TECHNICAL NOTES:
- Only use lungs that have been classified as 'fit for human consumption'.
- Disinfect equipment and work surfaces thoroughly after the dissection using a disinfectant such as Vikron.
- Do not store dissecting material in the same place as food that will be consumed.
- Use a sheep lung or pluck to reduce religious concerns.
- Have an alternative activity for students who do not want to perform a dissection.
- The students should wash their hands after the investigation.

METHOD:

To be done in advance by the teacher
Set-up optional demo: Use some rubber tubing and a foot pump to inflate one set of lungs to demonstrate breathing action.

STUDENTS:

1. Observe the lungs or pluck you have been given. What do they look like? Use a magnifying lens to examine the surface of the lungs.
2. Press down on the surface of the lungs. What do they feel like?
3. If the trachea (windpipe) is present then observe this structure. What does it look like? What does it feel like?
4. Use the scalpel to carefully cut one of the lungs open like a book. Use the magnifying lens to observe the inside of the lungs. What does it look like? What does it feel like? Draw your observations.

DATA COLLECTION IDEAS:
The students can make detailed, annotated drawings of their observations.

DIFFERENTIATION:
- **Decrease the challenge:** The students can be given diagram-based instructions to follow while performing the dissection.
- **Increase the challenge:** The students can perform additional observations of the lungs for example cutting off a piece of the lungs and adding it to a beaker of water to see that it floats, or preparing a microscope slide of a thin piece of the lungs.

USEFUL QUESTIONS TO ASK THE STUDENTS:
1. What did the lungs and trachea feel like? Why do you think they have this particular structure?
2. What did the inside of the lungs look like? Why do you think they have this structure?
3. What effect do you think smoking would have on the appearance and texture of the lungs?

HOMEWORK:
The students can research the effect of smoking on the lungs and other parts of the breathing system.

EXPERIMENT 4

Observation: Are all fats the same?

LEARNING OBJECTIVES:
Extract the fats from different foods and identify the saturated and unsaturated fats.

INTRODUCTION:
The students use denatured alcohol to extract the fats from different foods and then examine the extracted fats to identify whether they are saturated or unsaturated fats.

USEFUL PRIOR WORK:
The students should know that fats are found in some foods and that there are two different types of fats, saturated and unsaturated.

BACKGROUND SCIENCE:
Fats (lipids) are an essential food group. Fats are used for many important processes in the human body including the formation of cell walls and protecting internal organs. Fats come in two forms, saturated and unsaturated fats. Fats are formed from carbon and hydrogen atoms. The carbon atoms form the backbone of the fat and the hydrogen atoms attach to the carbon atoms. Each carbon atom can have a maximum of four bonds. If the carbon atoms in the backbone are attached to each other with a single bond then they have two bonds left to attach to hydrogen atoms. This is a saturated fat as the carbons are 'saturated' with hydrogen atoms. If the carbon atoms in the backbone are attached to each other with double bonds, then they only have one or zero bonds left for the hydrogen atoms. This is an unsaturated fat, as it is not saturated with hydrogen atoms. Saturated fats tend to be solid and unsaturated fats tend to be liquids at room temperature. Generally, unsaturated fats are better for you than saturated fats. In this investigation, the fats in the chocolate chips are saturated fats and the fats in the crisps and sunflower seeds are unsaturated fats.

NATIONAL CURRICULUM LINKS:

Nutrition and digestion:
- content of a healthy human diet: carbohydrates, lipids (fats and oils), proteins, vitamins, minerals, dietary fibre and water, and why each is needed
- the consequences of imbalances in the diet, including obesity, starvation and deficiency diseases.

MATERIALS NEEDED:
Chocolate chips, ready salted crisps, sunflower seeds, denatured alcohol, Petri dishes, measuring cylinders, beakers, balance, glass rods, eye protection, blender.

SAFETY AND TECHNICAL NOTES:
- This investigation needs to be carried out over two days.
- Dark chocolate chips work best for this investigation as they have a higher fat content.
- Denatured alcohol is flammable so should be kept away from all naked flames.
- The students should wear eye protection for this investigation.
- Be aware of any allergies and remind the students not to consume any of the food they're using.

METHOD:

To be done in advance by the teacher
Blend the chocolate chips, the sunflower seeds and the crisps so they are as fine a texture as possible.

STUDENTS:

1. Choose the first food you will be testing. Label a beaker with the name of the food.
2. Measure 5g of the food and then add it to the beaker.
3. Weigh the beaker that contains the food. Record the result.
4. Add 10ml of denatured alcohol to the beaker. Stir with a glass rod. Leave the beaker for one minute.
5. Label a Petri dish with the name of the food you are testing. Carefully pour the denatured alcohol from the beaker into the Petri dish, keeping the food in the beaker.
6. Place the beaker and the Petri dish somewhere safe to allow the denatured alcohol to evaporate overnight.
7. Repeat steps 1–6 for the rest of the foods you are testing.
8. Next day: observe the extracted fats in the Petri dishes. Record your observations.
9. Weigh each of your beakers. Use this result to calculate how much fat has been extracted from the food. (Minus this result from your first result.) Record your results.

DATA COLLECTION IDEAS:

Food	Observations	Mass at the start (g)	Mass at the end (g)	Fat extracted (g)

DIFFERENTIATION:
- **Decrease the challenge:** The students can work in groups with each group testing one food.
- **Increase the challenge:** The students can calculate the percentage of fat extracted from each food by dividing the weight lost from the food by the original weight of the food and multiplying this by 100.

USEFUL QUESTIONS TO ASK THE STUDENTS:
1. What observations did you make of the extracted fats?
2. Which fats were saturated and unsaturated? What does this tell us about those foods?
3. How much fat was extracted from each food? What does this tell us about those foods?

HOMEWORK:
The students can conduct a 'fat survey' of different foods by looking at the nutritional information labels and recording the saturated and unsaturated fat quantities.

EXPERIMENT 6

Observation: How do apples decay?

LEARNING OBJECTIVES:
Observe how slices of apple decay under different conditions.

INTRODUCTION:
The students cut apples into slices and place them under different conditions in order to see if and how they decay.

USEFUL PRIOR WORK:
The students should know that food can decay due to the presence of bacteria and fungi.

BACKGROUND SCIENCE:
If food is left out in the open for a long period of time it will begin to spoil. This is due to the presence of bacteria and fungi, which break down food. The food may look and taste different but can also contain harmful microorganisms that can make you unwell. In the case of apples, the inside of the apple will usually turn brown quite quickly if it is exposed to the air due to the process of oxidation. This is when oxygen from the air reacts with enzymes in the apple, leading to the deposition of brown coloured chemicals. Apples can also suffer from desiccation. This is where the apple loses water to the air and begins to shrivel up. There are methods that will reduce the rate of decay in apples. These involve either preventing the apple from coming into contact with the air or preventing the growth of microorganisms by using a substance with anti-microbial properties.

NATIONAL CURRICULUM LINKS:

Cellular respiration
- aerobic and anaerobic respiration in living organisms, including the breakdown of organic molecules to enable all the other chemical processes necessary for life
- the process of anaerobic respiration in humans and micro-organisms, including fermentation, and a word summary for anaerobic respiration.

MATERIALS NEEDED:
Apples, knife, white tiles, beakers, cling film, vinegar, lemon juice, fridge or other cold location, digital camera (optional)

SAFETY AND TECHNICAL NOTES:
- Remind the students not to consume the apples.
- Label the apples that are kept in the fridge as 'not for consumption'.
- Vinegar is an irritant.
- The students should wash their hands after the investigation.
- The students should cut up the apples only when they are ready to begin the investigation as they can begin to turn brown very quickly.

METHOD:

To be done in advance by the teacher
Ensure there is a suitable space for the 'cold' apple slices to be kept.

STUDENTS:

1. Cut your apple into five pieces. Try to make them roughly the same size.
2. Wrap one piece of apple in cling film.
3. Put one piece of apple in a beaker and pour in enough vinegar to cover the apple.
4. Put one piece of apple in a beaker and pour in enough lemon juice to cover the apple.
5. Place one piece of apple onto a white tile.
6. Put one piece of apple onto a white tile and place this into a fridge.
7. Observe the pieces of apple over the next week and note down your observations.

DATA COLLECTION IDEAS:
The students can take photographs of the apples and make notes on their observations.

DIFFERENTIATION:
- **Decrease the challenge:** The students can work in groups with each group investigating one of the methods in the investigation.
- **Increase the challenge:** The students can carry out a more systematic investigation by using apple slices of the same mass.

USEFUL QUESTIONS TO ASK THE STUDENTS:
1. Which method do you think will preserve the apple most effectively? Why do you think this?
2. What happened to the apple slices in the investigation? Why do you think this happened?
3. What other considerations would you need to take into account when preserving apple slices?

HOMEWORK:
The students can look at food items they have at home, for example fruit juice, bread, yogurt, and see what preservatives they can find on the ingredients list.

EXPERIMENT 7

Fair testing: Is salt a good preserver of food?

LEARNING OBJECTIVES:
Investigate how the concentration of salt affects how well it preserves food.

INTRODUCTION:
The students will use salt solutions of different concentrations to act as a preservative on peas.

USEFUL PRIOR WORK:
The students should know that food can decay due to the presence of bacteria and fungi.

BACKGROUND SCIENCE:
Salt has been used as a preservative for food since ancient times. Before the days of refrigeration and freezing, food had to be preserved using substances such as salt, sugar and vinegar. Food that has not been preserved will spoil quickly as the bacteria present will quickly multiple. This will not be obvious immediately though as the food may not look or smell any different. Over time the appearance and smell of the food may alter and visible mould may be present. Salt works as a preservative of food by removing the water from food, therefore making the conditions unsuitable for bacteria and fungi to multiply. The downside of using salt as a preservative is that high levels of salt in our diet are harmful and salt will alter the taste of the food.

NATIONAL CURRICULUM LINKS:

Nutrition and digestion
- content of a healthy human diet: carbohydrates, lipids (fats and oils), proteins, vitamins, minerals, dietary fibre and water, and why each is needed.

MATERIALS NEEDED:
Tinned peas in water (not salt water), salt, balance, test tubes, test-tube racks, measuring cylinders, measuring spoons, bowl or beakers, test tube stoppers or cotton wool, labels.

SAFETY AND TECHNICAL NOTES:
- Remind the students not to consume the peas.
- The students should wash their hands after the investigation.
- Use water from the hot tap for this investigation.
- This investigation should be carried out over a week.
- Be aware of any allergies.

METHOD:

To be done in advance by the teacher
Drain the tinned peas and place them in a bowl or beaker.

STUDENTS:

1 Set up five test tubes in a test-tube rack. Label the test tubes A–E.
2 Add five peas to each test tube.
3 Add 10cm^3 of hot water from the hot water tap to each test tube.
4 Add 1/4 teaspoon of salt to test tube B.
5 Add 1/2 teaspoon of salt to test tube C.
6 Add 3/4 teaspoon of salt to test tube D.
7 Add 1 teaspoon of salt to test tube E.
8 Place a test tube stopper or piece of cotton wool into the top of each test tube.
9 Place the test-tube rack somewhere warm and dry.
10 Observe the test tubes over the next few days and make notes on your observations.

DATA COLLECTION IDEAS:
The students can take photographs of the peas and make notes of their observations.

DIFFERENTIATION:
- **Decrease the challenge:** The students can work in groups with each group investigating one concentration of salt.
- **Increase the challenge:** The students could also carry out the investigation with dried peas to see if there is any difference in the results.

USEFUL QUESTIONS TO ASK THE STUDENTS:
1 What happened to the peas in the investigation? Why do you think this happened?
2 Why did we not add any salt to test tube A?
3 Why do you think salt acts as a preservative for food?

HOMEWORK:
The students can investigate the health risks associated with high levels of salt in our diet.

EXPERIMENT 8

Fair testing: How can plants use wind to reproduce?

LEARNING OBJECTIVES:
Investigate the factors that affect the dispersal of wind-dispersed seeds.

INTRODUCTION:
The students carry out an investigation into the dispersal of seeds by wind by making model sycamore seeds and testing them under different conditions.

USEFUL PRIOR WORK:
The students should know that some plants have seeds that can be dispersed by the wind.

BACKGROUND SCIENCE:
As plants are stationary organisms they need to be able to disperse their seeds. Dispersal of seeds is beneficial for plants as the further the seeds travel from the parent plant, the more likely they are to survive. This is because there will be less competition for resources between the parent plant and the offspring. Spreading seeds over a wide area also helps to reduce the risk of disease taking hold and spreading and it encourages predators to cover a larger area. All of these factors help to increase the likelihood of the offspring surviving and therefore helps to ensure the survival of the species. Wind is one way some plants disperse their seeds. Examples include sycamores and dandelions. Typically, the lighter the seed and the more aerodynamic the seed, the further the seed will travel. In this investigation a paper gyroscope (helicopter) is used as a model for a sycamore seed.

NATIONAL CURRICULUM LINKS:

Reproduction
- reproduction in plants, including flower structure, wind and insect pollination, fertilisation, seed and fruit formation and dispersal, including quantitative investigation of some dispersal mechanisms.

MATERIALS NEEDED:
Paper, paper helicopter templates with different sized blades, paperclips, metre rulers, electric fans, timers, scissors.

SAFETY AND TECHNICAL NOTES:
- The students should not climb on any furniture when dropping their seeds.
- Have a real sycamore seed to show the students if possible.
- The paperclip helps to stabilise the paper helicopter.

METHOD:

To be done in advance by the teacher
Have enough copies of the paper helicopter templates for the students.

STUDENTS:

1. Cut out your paper helicopter template and fold into shape. Add a paperclip to the bottom of your paper helicopter. This is your model sycamore seed.
2. Set up your testing zone. Place the fan onto a desk and use the metre ruler to measure one metre away from the fan. This will be where you will drop your seed. Make sure you drop the seed from the same height each time.
3. Turn on the fan and drop the seed. Time how long it takes for the seed to fall to the ground and measure how far the seed travelled. Record your results.
4. Repeat the investigation three times and take an average of your results.
5. Repeat the investigation with the other paper helicopter templates.

DATA COLLECTION IDEAS:

Length of blade (cm)	Time taken (s)			Average (s)
	Trial 1	Trial 2	Trial 3	

DIFFERENTIATION:

- **Decrease the challenge:** The students can work in groups with each group investigating one length of helicopter blade. The results can then be pooled together at the end of the investigation.
- **Increase the challenge:** The students could choose their own variable to investigate, for example, height the seed is dropped from, mass of the seed etc.

USEFUL QUESTIONS TO ASK THE STUDENTS:

1. What are the advantages and disadvantages of seeds being dispersed by wind?
2. What happened to the time taken and distance travelled when you increased the size of the blades? Why do you think this happened?
3. How would having larger 'wings' on its seed potentially benefit a sycamore tree?

HOMEWORK:

The students can research one other type of seed dispersal and find out which plants use that method.

EXPERIMENT 9

Fair testing:
Are there enzymes in our liver?

LEARNING OBJECTIVES:
Prove that liver contains an enzyme.

INTRODUCTION:
The students use hydrogen peroxide in order to test for the presence of enzymes in liver.

USEFUL PRIOR WORK:
The students should know what enzymes are and that they are found in the human body.

BACKGROUND SCIENCE:
Enzymes are biological catalysts. A catalyst is something that speeds up the rate of a chemical reaction without being used up itself in the reaction. Enzymes are proteins that are folded into a particular shape and have an area called an active site. The molecule the enzyme works on (the substrate) fits into this active site. This means that enzymes are specific to a particular molecule and only that particular molecule will fit into the active site. Enzymes either join two particular molecules together (anabolism) or break a molecule apart into two molecules (catabolism). As enzymes are proteins they need specific conditions (referred to as optimum conditions) in order to be able to work. The most important are temperature and pH. If these conditions differ too much from the optimum conditions then the active site can deform and the enzyme is no longer able to work. For human enzymes, the optimum temperature to work is 37°C. The liver contains the enzyme catalase that breaks down hydrogen peroxide into water and oxygen.

NATIONAL CURRICULUM LINKS:

Nutrition and digestion
- the tissues and organs of the human digestive system, including adaptations to function and how the digestive system digests food (enzymes simply as biological catalysts).

MATERIALS NEEDED:
Lamb's liver, test tubes, test-tube racks, hydrogen peroxide of five different concentrations, measuring cylinders, timers, Bunsen burners, splints, eye protection.

SAFETY AND TECHNICAL NOTES:
- Use a range of hydrogen peroxide concentrations for this investigation. Concentrations less than 18vol are low hazard. Concentrations between 18vol and 28vol are irritants.
- Do not use concentrations of hydrogen peroxide higher than 28vol.
- The students should wear eye protection for this investigation.
- The students should immediately wash off any hydrogen peroxide that comes into contact with their skin.
- Use liver from lambs in order to reduce religious concerns.
- Some students may object to handling liver so an alternative activity should be available.

METHOD:

To be done in advance by the teacher
Prepare the different concentrations of hydrogen peroxide that will be used in the investigation. Cut the liver up into small, roughly equal-sized pieces.

STUDENTS:

1. Set up five test tubes into a test tube rack. Set up a Bunsen burner and place it on the safety flame until you need to use it.
2. Add 25cm^3 of the first hydrogen peroxide concentration you are testing to a test tube.
3. Put your Bunsen burner onto the blue flame and light a splint in the flame. Blow out the flame so you have a glowing splint.
4. Place a piece of liver into the test tube then place the glowing splint into the top of the test tube. Time how long it takes the splint to relight.
5. Repeat the investigation with the rest of the concentrations of hydrogen peroxide.

DATA COLLECTION IDEAS:

Concentration of hydrogen peroxide	Time taken to relight (s)

DIFFERENTIATION:

- **Decrease the challenge:** The students can work in groups and investigate one concentration of hydrogen peroxide each. The results can then be pooled at the end of the investigation.
- **Increase the challenge:** The students can boil the liver and repeat the investigation in order to compare the results.

USEFUL QUESTIONS TO ASK THE STUDENTS:

1. What did you observe when the liver was added to the hydrogen peroxide? What did you observe when the glowing splint was added to the test tube? What does this prove?
2. Why do you think the speed of the reaction eventually stopped increasing?
3. What is the role of the liver in the human body?

HOMEWORK:

The students can draw a graph of their results.

EXPERIMENT 10

Fair testing: What is the best food to take with you when climbing a mountain?

LEARNING OBJECTIVES:
Investigate the energy levels in different foods.

INTRODUCTION:
The students compare the energy levels of different foods by burning samples of the food and measuring the resulting temperature increase of water.

USEFUL PRIOR WORK:
The students should be able to use a Bunsen burner.

BACKGROUND SCIENCE:
The SI units for energy levels in food are joules, however calories tend to be used in everyday terminology. A calorie is the amount of energy required to raise $1cm^3$ of water by 1°C. Certain foods contain higher levels of energy than other foods. Typically, foods that contain large amounts of carbohydrates and sugars contain high levels of energy. This is because fats and sugars are the preferred 'fuel' for the human body to use in the process of respiration (the release of energy from food). When we perform higher levels of activity the body requires more energy for the process of respiration. Foods that have high levels of energy that can be released quickly are the best foods for when you require a short burst of energy. Slow energy releasing foods are best for when you need a long, sustained supply of energy.

NATIONAL CURRICULUM LINKS:

Nutrition and digestion
- content of a healthy human diet: carbohydrates, lipids (fats and oils), proteins, vitamins, minerals, dietary fibre and water, and why each is needed
- calculations of energy requirements in a healthy daily diet
- the consequences of imbalances in the diet, including obesity, starvation and deficiency diseases.

MATERIALS NEEDED:
A selection of foods to test – (for example, crisps, bread, crackers, fruit, cereal, pasta, cheese, biscuits), Bunsen burners, heat proof mats, boiling tubes, clamp stands, boss and clamps, measuring cylinders, thermometers, balance, mounted needles, tongs, eye protection, water.

SAFETY AND TECHNICAL NOTES:
- Avoid using nuts because of allergies.
- Use tongs for food samples that cannot be impaled with the mounted needle.
- The students should wear eye protection for the investigation.
- Remind the students that the bottom of the boiling tube will become very hot so they should not touch it.

- Remind the students to take care when placing food onto the mounted needle.
- Remind the students not to consume any of the food samples and be aware of allergies.

METHOD:

To be done in advance by the teacher
Prepare the food samples to be tested. Ensure they are roughly equal sized pieces, about 1cm^3 will be sufficient.

STUDENTS:

1. Set up your boss and clamp stand and Bunsen burner. Put your Bunsen burner onto the safety flame until it is needed.
2. Add 25cm of water to the boiling tube and place it into the clamp.
3. Take the temperature of the water and record this in your results table.
4. Select the first piece of food you will be testing. Use the balance to find its mass and record this in your results table.
5. Carefully place the food onto the mounted needle or use the tongs if this is not possible.
6. Hold the food in the Bunsen burner flame until it catches alight.
7. Immediately place the burning food under the boiling tube so that the flame is directly underneath the boiling tube. The flame does not have to touch the boiling tube.
8. Hold the food under the boiling tube until the food has burnt away. If the flame goes out then quickly relight it using the Bunsen burner and place it back under the boiling tube.
9. When the food has burnt away, take the temperature of the water again and record this in your results table.
10. Repeat the investigation with the rest of the food samples.

DATA COLLECTION IDEAS:

Food	Temp. of water at the start (°C)	Temp. of water at the end (°C)	Increase in temp. of water (°C)

DIFFERENTIATION:
- **Decrease the challenge:** The students can work in groups with each group investigating one food sample. The results can then be pooled together at the end of the investigation.
- **Increase the challenge:** The students can conduct a more accurate investigation by using a calorimeter if one is available.

USEFUL QUESTIONS TO ASK THE STUDENTS:
1. Which foods would you take on a mountain trek? Why is this?
2. Did every group get the same results for each food sample? Why do you think this was?
3. Why do you think energy levels on food packages are given per 100g?

HOMEWORK:
The students can research what food and other items are taken on famous climbs such as Mount Everest and what other factors need to be taken into consideration, for example weight and size.

EXPERIMENT 11

Fair testing: Which is the most dangerous sea to swim in if you are bleeding?

LEARNING OBJECTIVES:
Determine in which sea a shark would find a bleeding diver first.

INTRODUCTION:
The students calculate the rate of diffusion in water of different temperatures in order to simulate a shark attack.

USEFUL PRIOR WORK:
The students should know what diffusion is and how it occurs.

BACKGROUND SCIENCE:
Diffusion is the movement of particles from an area of high concentration to an area of low concentration. Diffusion can happen in both liquids and gases. All particles have a certain level of kinetic (movement) energy that allows them to move around randomly. There are certain factors that can affect the rate at which diffusion happens, for example temperature and stirring. If you increase the temperature you provide the particles with more kinetic energy, allowing them to move around faster and therefore diffuse faster. With stirring the particles are forcibly moved around therefore making the particles diffuse faster. Diffusion will eventually happen in all liquids and gases, even very cold ones, it will just happen very slowly.

NATIONAL CURRICULUM LINKS:

Cells and organisation
- the role of diffusion in the movement of materials in and between cells.

Pure and impure substances
- diffusion in terms of the particle model.

MATERIALS NEEDED:
Water troughs, red food colouring, model sharks, timers, thermometers, droppers, Blu Tack.

SAFETY AND TECHNICAL NOTES:

- Use three 'seas' for this experiment. Coral Sea (Australia) – between 25°C and 30°C, North Sea (England) – between 10°C and 15°C, and Bering Sea (Russia) – between 1°C and 5°C.
- Water from the hot tap is sufficient for this investigation.
- Keep water away from electrical devices.
- Clear up any water spills immediately.

METHOD:

To be done in advance by the teacher
Prepare the model sharks. These can be a simple item such as a paperclip or can be fashioned to look like a shark using plasticine.

STUDENTS:

1 Prepare your first 'sea'. Use the water troughs and make sure the temperature of the sea falls within the required range.
2 Place your shark at the far end of your trough or beaker. Hold it in place with Blu Tack.
3 Add three drops of red food colouring to the other end of the trough or beaker and start your timer. When the red food colouring has reached your shark stop the timer.
4 Record the time in your results table.
5 Empty your water trough and repeat the investigation for the other two seas.

DATA COLLECTION IDEAS:

Temp. of the sea (°C)	Time taken for blood to reach the shark (s)

DIFFERENTIATION:
- **Decrease the challenge:** The seas can be made for the students by using large beakers of water placed into water baths.
- **Increase the challenge:** The students can investigate the effect of waves by agitating the water by different amounts and seeing how this affects the rate of diffusion.

USEFUL QUESTIONS TO ASK THE STUDENTS:
1 In which sea would the shark find the diver first? Why do you think this would happen?
2 What other factors might help the shark find the diver?
3 What do you think divers should do to avoid being attacked by sharks?

HOMEWORK:
The students can prepare a safety poster for display at beaches informing swimmers how to avoid shark attacks.

EXPERIMENT 12

Fair testing:
How quickly will our muscles tire?

LEARNING OBJECTIVES:
Investigate muscle fatigue in our arm muscles.

INTRODUCTION:
The students investigate how arm muscles tire by performing a simple exercise in a set period of time.

USEFUL PRIOR WORK:
The students should know what muscles are and their role in the body.

BACKGROUND SCIENCE:
Muscles are a type of tissue found in the human body. There are three different types of muscle, smooth (e.g. intestinal muscle), cardiac (found in the heart) and skeletal (e.g. biceps). The only muscles we have conscious control over are our skeletal muscles. Muscles are connected to the bones in our body by tissues called tendons. Muscles can either contract or relax which then results in the movement of the bones. Muscle fatigue occurs when the muscle is unable to generate sufficient force to move the bone. Muscle fatigue often occurs when the same repetitive action is performed by a muscle or set of muscles and can be caused by a lack of fuel (energy released from food) required by the muscle or a build-up of toxic materials in the muscles.

NATIONAL CURRICULUM LINKS:

The skeletal and muscular systems
- biomechanics – the interaction between skeleton and muscles, including the measurement of force exerted by different muscles
- the function of muscles and examples of antagonistic muscles.

MATERIALS NEEDED:
Timers, small weights such as a small bag of sand or a cricket ball.

SAFETY AND TECHNICAL NOTES:
- Make sure that the weight is not too heavy for the students.
- The students should work in small groups for this investigation.

METHOD:

To be done in advance by the teacher
Prepare the weights the students will be using in the investigation.

STUDENTS:

1. Decide who will be tested first. Have them place their forearm flat onto the table.
2. Place the weight into their hand so they can hold it firmly.

3 Start the timer and have the person raise the weight to their shoulder by bending their elbow. Their elbow should not come off the table. Record how many times they can do this in one minute.
4 When one minute has passed have the person rest their arm for one minute before continuing.
5 Repeat steps three and four two more times.
6 Repeat the investigation for the rest of the people in the group.

DATA COLLECTION IDEAS:

Attempt	No. of repetitions

DIFFERENTIATION:
- **Decrease the challenge:** The students can be given help with the timings for the investigation.
- **Increase the challenge:** The students could compare muscle fatigue in both arms to see if there is any difference between their dominant and non-dominant hands.

USEFUL QUESTIONS TO ASK THE STUDENTS:
1 What did you observe in your results? Why do you think this happened?
2 How did your arm muscles feel during the investigation?
3 What could we do to improve how soon our muscles fatigue?

HOMEWORK:
The students can produce a graph of the results for their group.

EXPERIMENT 13

Fair testing: Can we speed up the rate of photosynthesis?

LEARNING OBJECTIVES:
Investigate the effect of light on the rate of photosynthesis.

INTRODUCTION:
The students punch out discs from leaves and float them in a syringe containing sodium hydrogen carbonate solution and observe them rising and falling as oxygen is released during photosynthesis.

USEFUL PRIOR WORK:
The students should know the reactants and products of photosynthesis.

BACKGROUND SCIENCE:
A leaf disc is a small, circular shape cut out from a normal leaf. When leaf discs are placed into a liquid they will initially float as they contain spaces filled with air. However, as the leaf disc takes up the liquid it is floating in those air spaces will fill up and the leaf disc will sink. If the leaf disc is placed into a solution containing sodium hydrogen carbonate and there is a nearby light source, then the leaf disc will start photosynthesising (the carbon in the bicarbonate acts as the carbon source for the photosynthesis) and will eventually float again due to the oxygen being produced. The rate the leaf discs rise can be used as a measure of photosynthesis.

NATIONAL CURRICULUM LINKS:

Photosynthesis
- the reactants in, and products of, photosynthesis, and a word summary for photosynthesis
- the dependence of almost all life on Earth on the ability of photosynthetic organisms, such as plants and algae, to use sunlight in photosynthesis to build organic molecules that are an essential energy store and to maintain levels of oxygen and carbon dioxide in the atmosphere
- the adaptations of leaves for photosynthesis.

MATERIALS NEEDED:
Lamps, suitable plant leaves for making leaf discs, 10cm^3 syringes, 0.2M sodium hydrogen carbonate solution, cork borers, rulers, timers.

SAFETY AND TECHNICAL NOTES:

- Suitable plants for this investigation include ivy, radish and clover. The plants used should be healthy and growing well.
- A cork borer can be used to produce the leaf discs.

METHOD:

To be done in advance by the teacher
Prepare the leaf discs if the students will not be doing this themselves.

STUDENTS:

1. Use a cork borer to cut five discs from a leaf.
2. Remove the plunger from the syringe. Carefully place the leaf discs inside the syringe. Replace the plunger.
3. Draw up 10cm^3 of the sodium hydrogen carbonate solution into the syringe. Tap the syringe gently to remove any air bubbles. The leaf discs should eventually sink to the bottom of the syringe.
4. Stand the syringe up on its plunger and place the lamp 5cm from the syringe.
5. Start the timer and record how long it takes each leaf disc to float to the top of the syringe.
6. Repeat the investigation two more times with the lamp 10cm and 20cm from the syringe.

DATA COLLECTION IDEAS:

Distance of lamp from plant (cm)	Time taken for leaf disc to float (s)

DIFFERENTIATION:

- **Decrease the challenge:** The students can put just one leaf disc into each syringe.
- **Increase the challenge:** The students can investigate a wider range of distances from the lamp.

USEFUL QUESTIONS TO ASK THE STUDENTS:

1. Why did the leaf discs sink and then rise in the syringe?
2. What happened when the lamp was moved further away from the syringe? Why do you think this happened?
3. Why do you think the leaf discs in the same syringe floated at different times?

HOMEWORK:
The students can produce a graph of their results.

EXPERIMENT 14

Pattern seeking: Where do daisies grow?

LEARNING OBJECTIVES:
Investigate whether more daisies grow in the middle or edge of the school field.

INTRODUCTION:
The students conduct a survey to find out whether more daisies are growing in the centre of the school field compared with the edges of the school field.

USEFUL PRIOR WORK:
The students should know the factors and conditions plants need in order to grow.

BACKGROUND SCIENCE:
Quadrats are small plastic squares used in environmental surveys. The square is randomly thrown and the number or estimated percentage of different species found within the quadrat are counted. This type of survey is called a sampling survey as it only covers a small area or 'sample' of the area being studied. The results from the quadrats are extrapolated to cover the rest of the area as it is assumed that whatever is found within the quadrats will be found within the rest of the area being studied. Usually, 10% is considered to be a suitable sample size when conducting an environmental survey using quadrats. Factors that will affect the number of plants in a given area are temperature, light levels, moisture content and pH of the soil and the presence of any predators.

NATIONAL CURRICULUM LINKS:

Photosynthesis
- the reactants in, and products of, photosynthesis, and a word summary for photosynthesis.

Relationships in an ecosystem
- how organisms affect, and are affected by, their environment, including the accumulation of toxic materials.

MATERIALS NEEDED:
Quadrats or plastic hoops, data-loggers (optional).

SAFETY AND TECHNICAL NOTES:
- Demonstrate to the students how to throw the quadrats or hoops safely.
- Instruct the students on where they are allowed to go for the investigation.
- The students should aim to do five quadrats for the middle of the field and five quadrats for the edge of the field.

METHOD:

To be done in advance by the teacher
Select where the students will be carrying out the investigation.

STUDENTS:

1 Start your investigation in the middle of the field.
2 Throw your quadrat randomly onto the ground. Count how many daisies are present in the quadrat.
3 Repeat four more times for the middle of the field. Try to cover a wide area of the field.
4 Move to the edge of the field and repeat your investigation. Make sure you do five quadrats.
5 If you are using a data-logger, record the light levels, temperature and soil moisture levels in the middle of the field and the edge of the field.

DATA COLLECTION IDEAS:

Edge of field		Middle of field	
Quadrat number	Number of daisies	Quadrat number	Number of daisies
Average			

DIFFERENTIATION:

- **Decrease the challenge:** The students could be helped with deciding where to throw the quadrats.
- **Increase the challenge:** The students could also investigate other factors such as light levels, moisture levels and temperature in the middle and edges of the field using a data-logger.

USEFUL QUESTIONS TO ASK THE STUDENTS:

1 Did you find any difference in the number of daisies in the middle of the field compared with the edge of the field? Why do you think this was?
2 What factors would affect how many daisies grow on the field?
3 Do you think you would find the same pattern of daisies in the other seasons of the year?

HOMEWORK:

The students can research how to carry out other types of environmental surveys, for example pitfall traps and capture, mark, release.

EXPERIMENT 15

Pattern seeking:
Do taller people have larger hands?

LEARNING OBJECTIVES:
Investigate whether taller people have a longer handspan than shorter people.

INTRODUCTION:
The students conduct a class survey by measuring each other's height and handspans. The results can then be pooled in order to produce a class graph.

USEFUL PRIOR WORK:
The students should be able to use simple measuring devices such as tape-measures.

BACKGROUND SCIENCE:
The human body is generally in proportion in terms of factors such as bone length. One reason for this is that our genes (found in DNA) contribute to the length that bones will grow in our bodies. Other factors such as health and diet can influence the development of bones. Again, these effects would be similar across the human body, meaning that bones would still be in proportion to each other. This type of relationship is called positive correlation. This means that as one variable increases, for example height, another variable, for example handspan, also increases. If the two variables increased at exactly the same proportion for each individual in the sample, then the result would be perfect positive correlation, with a perfectly straight line of best fit. However, this is unlikely to happen and instead a more general positive correlation is likely to be found.

NATIONAL CURRICULUM LINKS:

Inheritance, chromosomes, DNA and genes
- heredity as the process by which genetic information is transmitted from one generation to the next
- the variation between individuals within a species being continuous or discontinuous, to include measurement and graphical representation of variation
- the variation between species and between individuals of the same species means some organisms compete more successfully, which can drive natural selection.

MATERIALS NEEDED:
Tape-measures.

SAFETY AND TECHNICAL NOTES:
- Have the children work in small groups and take the measurements for everyone in their group. The results of the different groups can then be added to the class graph.
- Instruct the children to measure the handspan while the hand is spread out as much as possible.
- Measuring someone while they are stood against a wall will help to make the measuring of height more accurate.

METHOD:

To be done in advance by the teacher
Have a class graph prepared – either drawn onto a white board or projected onto a whiteboard.

STUDENTS:

1. Use the tape-measure to measure the height of everyone in your group. Make sure they are stood straight and you hold the tape-measure taut.
2. Use the tape-measure to measure the handspan of everyone in your group. Make sure the person has their hand spread out and you hold the tape-measure taut.
3. Add your results to the class graph.

DATA COLLECTION IDEAS:
A class graph can be prepared. A line of best fit can be added to introduce the idea of correlation.

DIFFERENTIATION:
- **Decrease the challenge:** The students can be assisted with the measuring.
- **Increase the challenge:** The students can be encouraged to take more accurate measurements, for example in millimetres.

USEFUL QUESTIONS TO ASK THE STUDENTS:
1. Was there any pattern in our results? Why do you think this was?
2. What other factors might affect a person's height?
3. What other factors might affect a person's handspan?

HOMEWORK:
The students can research the medical condition rickets including its causes and its effects on bones.

EXPERIMENT 16

Pattern seeking: Do insects prefer to live in the light or the dark?

LEARNING OBJECTIVES:
Investigate if there are more insects in dark habitats or light habitats in the school grounds.

INTRODUCTION:
The students conduct a survey of the number and variety of insects living in the school grounds to determine which conditions they prefer – dark or light.

USEFUL PRIOR WORK:
The students should be able to use identification keys.

BACKGROUND SCIENCE:
A habitat is the specific location in an environment where a particular organism lives. Most organisms are adapted for the habitat in which they live, meaning that they will generally only survive in their preferred habitat and any changes to that habitat can lead to a decline of that species. In terms of insects, there are a number of different habitats in which they can be found. Some insects such as woodlice prefer dark and damp habitats, for example under logs. Other insects, such as solitary bees, prefer tunnels in the ground. Generally insects will prefer habitats that offer them protection from predators; these will typically be habitats that are not out in the open.

NATIONAL CURRICULUM LINKS:

Relationships in an ecosystem
- the interdependence of organisms in an ecosystem, including food webs and insect pollinated crops.

Inheritance, chromosomes, DNA and genes
- differences between species
- the variation between species and between individuals of the same species means some organisms compete more successfully, which can drive natural selection
- changes in the environment may leave individuals within a species, and some entire species, less well adapted to compete successfully and reproduce, which in turn may lead to extinction.

MATERIALS NEEDED:
Identification keys for common insects, magnifying lenses, data-logger with light sensor.

SAFETY AND TECHNICAL NOTES:
- Instruct the students on where they are allowed to go when conducting the survey.
- You may want to suggest some areas for the students to investigate, for example, in the grass on the school field, under a tree, under a hedge, etc.
- Remind the students to respect living organisms and to not remove the insects.
- The students should wash their hands after the investigation.

METHOD:

To be done in advance by the teacher
Set up the data-loggers and make sure the students are able to use them to record light levels.

STUDENTS:

1. Choose the first location you will be surveying. Record the location in your results table.
2. Use the data-logger to record the light levels in your chosen location.
3. Count how many insects are present in your chosen location. Use the identification key to identify which insects are living in your chosen location.
4. Repeat the investigation at different locations.

DATA COLLECTION IDEAS:

Location	No. of insects	Light levels

DIFFERENTIATION:
- **Decrease the challenge:** The students can be given a list of locations to survey.
- **Increase the challenge:** The students could also measure other factors such as temperature and moisture levels.

USEFUL QUESTIONS TO ASK THE STUDENTS:
1. In which locations did you find the most/least number of insects? Why do you think this was?
2. In which locations did you find the greatest/least variety of insects? Why do you think this was?
3. What other factors might affect where insects choose to live?

HOMEWORK:
The students could conduct an environmental survey at their own homes, for example an insect survey or bird survey.

EXPERIMENT 17

Pattern seeking: Can long legs jump further?

LEARNING OBJECTIVES:
Investigate whether people with longer legs jump further than people with shorter legs.

INTRODUCTION:
The students conduct a class survey comparing leg length with how far an individual can jump.

USEFUL PRIOR WORK:
The students should be able to use simple measuring equipment such as tape-measures.

BACKGROUND SCIENCE:
Generally speaking, individuals with longer legs will be able to jump further than those with shorter legs. This is due to the physics involved in jumping. A forward jump is a type of projectile motion activity and having a longer 'lever' in the form of a longer leg will usually allow the individual to jump further than someone with shorter legs. However, there are other factors that will affect how far a person jumps, such as how high they jump, how they swing their legs whilst jumping and whether they perform a stationary jump (jumping from a standing still position) or a running jump. External factors such as wind resistance and floor surface can also affect how far a person will jump.

NATIONAL CURRICULUM LINKS:

The skeletal and muscular systems
- biomechanics – the interaction between skeleton and muscles, including the measurement of force exerted by different muscles.

Inheritance, chromosomes, DNA and genes
- the variation between individuals within a species being continuous or discontinuous, to include measurement and graphical representation of variation
- the variation between species and between individuals of the same species means some organisms compete more successfully, which can drive natural selection.

MATERIALS NEEDED:
Tape-measures.

SAFETY AND TECHNICAL NOTES:
- Conduct this investigation in an open space such as a sports hall or playground.
- The students should wear suitable footwear for this investigation.
- The students should perform a 'stepping' jump rather than a both feet together jump.
- The students should perform a stationary jump rather than a running jump.
- Have the children work in small groups and take the measurements for everyone in their group. The results of the different groups can then be added to the class graph.

METHOD:

To be done in advance by the teacher
Have a class graph prepared – either drawn onto a whiteboard or projected onto a whiteboard.

STUDENTS:

1 Measure the leg length of everyone in your group. Start at the hip and measure down the outside of the leg. Hold the tape-measure taut. Record the results in your table.
2 Choose a starting point for your jumps. Have everyone in your group perform a stationary 'stepping' jump and measure how far they jumped. You may want to perform a practice jump first. Record the results in your table.
3 Add your results to the class graph.

DATA COLLECTION IDEAS:
A class graph can be prepared.

DIFFERENTIATION:
- **Decrease the challenge:** The students can be assisted with the measuring.
- **Increase the challenge:** The students can be encouraged to take more accurate measurements, for example, in millimetres.

USEFUL QUESTIONS TO ASK THE STUDENTS:
1 Was there any pattern in our results? Why do you think this was?
2 What other factors might affect how far a person can jump?
3 Do you think the results would be any different if we had performed a running jump? Why do you think this?

HOMEWORK:
The students can research the current world records for various Olympic jumping events such as the long jump and triple jump.

EXPERIMENT 18

Pattern seeking: Do our hearts beat faster when we work harder?

LEARNING OBJECTIVES:
Investigate if high impact exercise will increase our heart rate more than low impact exercise.

INTRODUCTION:
The students will work in groups to see the effect that different types of exercise has on their heart rate.

USEFUL PRIOR WORK:
The students should know what the role of the heart is in the human body.

BACKGROUND SCIENCE:
The heart is an organ responsible for pumping blood around the body. Useful products such as oxygen and digested food are carried in the blood to cells around the body and waste products such as carbon dioxide are carried to specific organs where they can be excreted. During exercise, the heart needs to beat faster so that it can supply oxygen and digested food to our muscles for the process of respiration. Muscle cells respire in order to produce energy (in the form of ATP). The more work the muscles are required to do, the more they will need to respire. During periods of increased respiration, waste products such as carbon dioxide are also produced at a faster rate. These products need to be removed from the body, requiring the heart to beat faster to transport them in the blood to the required excretory organs.

NATIONAL CURRICULUM LINKS:

Cellular respiration
- aerobic and anaerobic respiration in living organisms, including the breakdown of organic molecules to enable all the other chemical processes necessary for life
- a word summary for aerobic respiration.

MATERIALS NEEDED:
Timers, data-logger with pulse rate sensor (optional), exercise equipment, for example, skipping ropes (optional).

SAFETY AND TECHNICAL NOTES:
- This investigation should be carried out in an open space such as a sports hall or playground.
- The students should wear appropriate footwear for this investigation.
- Be aware of any health issues that affect students.
- Be sensitive to the needs of students who may not be comfortable exercising; consider placing them in a low-intensity exercise group.
- Data-loggers can be used for this investigation or the students can take their pulse the conventional way. You may wish to demonstrate this to remind students how to take their pulse.

- Exercise equipment could be used for this investigation. If used, be sure to observe standard safe practice.
- Keep exercise levels to those students would experience in a normal PE lesson.
- Types of exercise could include running on the spot, skipping with a rope, jumping jacks, squats, bouncing a ball, walking around the room.

METHOD:

To be done in advance by the teacher

Decide what types of exercise will be performed by each group of students. Divide the students into the required groups.

STUDENTS:

1 Take your pulse whilst you are sat down and resting. Record this in your table.
2 Perform your selected type of exercise for one minute. As soon as you have stopped exercising take your pulse again. Record this in your table.
3 Calculate the percentage increase in your heart rate for that type of exercise.
4 When everyone in your group has their results, calculate the average increase in heart rate for your group.
5 Compare that result with the results obtained from the other groups.

DATA COLLECTION IDEAS:

A class graph can be prepared.

DIFFERENTIATION:

- **Decrease the challenge:** The students can simply calculate how much their heart rate increased rather than the percentage increase.
- **Increase the challenge:** The students could also record how long it takes for their heart rate to return to their resting heart rate by taking their pulse every minute.

USEFUL QUESTIONS TO ASK THE STUDENTS:

1 Which type of exercise increased our heart rate the most/least? Why do you think this was?
2 Why does our heart need to beat faster when we exercise?
3 What other factors might have affected our results?

HOMEWORK:

The students could produce a leaflet aimed at young people informing them about how to have a healthy heart and why this is important.

EXPERIMENT 19

Pattern seeking: Are hand-dryers more hygienic than paper towels?

LEARNING OBJECTIVES:

Investigate whether it is more hygienic to dry our hands using a hand-dryer or paper towels.

INTRODUCTION:

The students compare how clean their hands are after washing them and drying them with either a hand-dryer or paper towels.

USEFUL PRIOR WORK:

The students should know what bacteria and viruses are, and that they can cause disease.

BACKGROUND SCIENCE:

Bacteria and viruses are examples of microorganisms that can cause disease. Bacteria are unicellular organisms, whereas viruses consist of DNA surrounded by a protein coat. Bacteria multiply using asexual reproduction whilst viruses invade other living cells and use the cells to produce more copies of the virus. Our skin is one place where large numbers of bacteria and viruses can be found. Not all of these will be harmful to our health but some could cause serious disease. Washing our hands regularly helps to reduce the number of harmful bacteria and viruses present on our hands. Factors that affect how well our hands are cleaned include the temperature of the water used, whether soap is used, how vigorously our hands are washed and the method used to dry our hands.

NATIONAL CURRICULUM LINKS:

Cells and organisation
- the structural adaptations of some unicellular organisms.

MATERIALS NEEDED:

Agar plates, sellotape, pen or pencil for writing on agar plate, paper towels, liquid soap, hand-dryer, access to sink, access to a hand-dryer.

SAFETY AND TECHNICAL NOTES:

- Have students work in pairs with one agar plate between them.
- The agar plates can be incubated at room temperature for 48 hours to allow the bacterial growth.
- Instruct the students not to open up the agar plates after the bacteria have been grown.

METHOD:

To be done in advance by the teacher

Have enough agar plates prepared for the students.

STUDENTS:

1. Draw a line down the middle of the agar plate to divide it into two halves. Label one half as 'paper towels' and the other half as 'hand-dryer'.
2. Decide if you will be drying your hands using a paper towel or hand-dryer. Wash your hands thoroughly and then dry them using your chosen method. You only need to test one hand so try not to touch anything else with one of your hands after you have dried them.
3. Use one hand to remove the lid off your agar plate. Use the fingers of your other hand to press very gently onto the agar.
4. Replace the lid of the agar plate. Have your partner do the same with their hand on the other side of the agar plate.
5. Place your agar plate somewhere safe and warm.
6. Observe your agar plate over the next few days to see what bacterial growth occurs.

DATA COLLECTION IDEAS:

The students can compare the agar plates produced and attempt to quantify how much bacteria is present on each plate.

DIFFERENTIATION:

- **Decrease the challenge:** The students can use separate agar plates for drying with paper towels and drying with a hand-dryer.
- **Increase the challenge:** The students can measure the bacterial growth present on the plates and produce averages for drying with paper towels and drying with a hand-dryer.

USEFUL QUESTIONS TO ASK THE STUDENTS:

1. Was there any difference in bacterial growth for hands dried with paper towels compared with hands dried with a hand-dryer? Is this what you expected?
2. What are the advantages and disadvantages of using paper towels/hand-dryers to dry your hands?
3. What other factors will affect how clean your hands are after washing them?

HOMEWORK:

The students can produce a poster showing proper hand washing technique.

EXPERIMENT 20

Classification and identification: Can you identify animal and plant cells just by looking at them?

LEARNING OBJECTIVES:
Correctly classify cells as either plant or animal cells.

INTRODUCTION:
The students observe slides of cells under a microscope and identify them as either plant or animal cells.

USEFUL PRIOR WORK:
The students should know the basic structure of animal and plant cells and how to use a microscope.

BACKGROUND SCIENCE:
Plant and animal cells are examples of eukaryotic cells. This means that they have membrane bound organelles including a membrane bound nucleus. Plant and animal cells have some structures in common including a nucleus, cell membrane, cytoplasm and mitochondria. Plant cells, however, have some additional structures that are not found in animal cells. These include a cell wall, which provides the plant with some rigidity, chloroplasts (only found in leaf cells that will be photosynthesising), which contain the chemical chlorophyll that is necessary for photosynthesis, and a vacuole filled with cell sap that takes up most of the space inside the plant cell. This vacuole helps to keep the cell turgid. These structures make up the general structure of animal and plant cells, however cells will become specialised in order to perform a specific job, for example a sperm cell or root hair cell. This means that the cells will have different overall structures.

NATIONAL CURRICULUM LINKS:

Cells and organisation
- cells as the fundamental unit of living organisms, including how to observe, interpret and record cell structure using a light microscope
- the functions of the cell wall, cell membrane, cytoplasm, nucleus, vacuole, mitochondria and chloroplasts
- the similarities and differences between plant and animal cells.

MATERIALS NEEDED:
A selection of prepared slides of both animal and plant cells, microscopes.

SAFETY AND TECHNICAL NOTES:
- Have a sharps bin for any slides that break.

METHOD:

To be done in advance by the teacher
You may want to make a handout showing different types of specialised cells for the students to use during their identification.

STUDENTS:

1. Select the first slide you will be examining.
2. Place the slide onto the microscope and adjust the magnification until you can view the cells.
3. Draw and label what you can see on your microscope slide. Classify the cell as either a plant cell or an animal cell. See if you can identify which type of animal or plant cell it is.
4. Repeat with the rest of the slides.

DATA COLLECTION IDEAS:
The students can make labelled drawings of their observations.

DIFFERENTIATION:
- **Decrease the challenge:** The students can be given photographs of different types of cells to aid them with their identification.
- **Increase the challenge:** The students can also try to identify what type of specialised cell they are observing.

USEFUL QUESTIONS TO ASK THE STUDENTS:
1. How were you able to identify which cells were plant cells and which cells were animal cells?
2. Why don't all plant/animal cells look the same as each other?
3. Why do plant cells need structures that animal cells do not have?

HOMEWORK:
The students could research the work of Robert Hooke on cells.

EXPERIMENT 21

Classification and identification: Can we classify leaves?

LEARNING OBJECTIVES:
Produce a classification key for the identification of leaves.

INTRODUCTION:
The students will collect a variety of leaves and then produce a classification key for their identification.

USEFUL PRIOR WORK:
The students should know what a classification key is and how to use one.

BACKGROUND SCIENCE:
Leaves can be classified by a number of different factors. The first level of classification is whether the leaf is simple or compound. A simple leaf is composed of one, single, undivided leaf growing from the node (the place where the leaf is attached to the stem), for example, oak leaves and banana leaves. A compound leaf is made up of a number of smaller leaflets attached to one bud growing from the node, for example, rose leaves and ash leaves. Leaves can also be classified by their overall shape, which includes ovate, obovate, oblong and elliptic. The edges of leaves can also be either entire, i.e. a smooth edge, or lobed, i.e. a jagged edge.

NATIONAL CURRICULUM LINKS:

Photosynthesis
- the adaptations of leaves for photosynthesis.

MATERIALS NEEDED:
A selection of different leaves, magnifying lenses, rulers, a selection of diagrams of different leaves or access to the Internet.

SAFETY AND TECHNICAL NOTES:
- Instruct the students on where they are allowed to go when collecting the leaves.
- Remind the students that leaves can also be collected from plants and bushes and not just trees.
- Remind the students not to pick any wildflowers.
- The students should wash their hands after the investigation.

METHOD:

To be done in advance by the teacher
Have a selection of diagrams of different named leaves for the students to use when identifying their leaves. Alternatively, have computers with access to the Internet for the students to use to identify their leaves.

STUDENTS:

1 Collect your sample of leaves. Try to collect at least eight different types of leaf.
2 Use the diagrams you have been given to identify the species of plant that your leaves came from. Write down the name of the plant they come from.
3 Start to produce your classification key. Think about what the leaves have in common and what is different about them. Practise your classification key on a spare piece of paper until you have managed to classify all of your leaves.
4 When you have produced your key, swap with another group and see if they can use your classification key to identify your leaves.

DATA COLLECTION IDEAS:
The students can produce a final version of their classification key.

DIFFERENTIATION:
- **Decrease the challenge:** The students can collect a smaller number of leaves.
- **Increase the challenge:** The students can add annotated drawings of the leaves to their classification key.

USEFUL QUESTIONS TO ASK THE STUDENTS:
1 Why is it useful to be able to classify different organisms?
2 Why do you think leaves come in different shapes?
3 What features of a leaf help with the process of photosynthesis?

HOMEWORK:
The students can produce a classification key for another type of organism, for example beetles. They can be provided with diagrams of different types of beetle in order to produce their classification key.

EXPERIMENT 22

Classification and identification: What are the best fruits and vegetables to eat when you have a cold?

LEARNING OBJECTIVES:
Identify which fruits and vegetables contain vitamin C.

INTRODUCTION:
The students test different fruits and vegetables in order to classify them as either containing vitamin C or not containing vitamin C.

USEFUL PRIOR WORK:
The students should know that vitamins are necessary for good health.

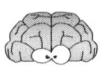

BACKGROUND SCIENCE:
Vitamin C, also known as ascorbic acid, is an essential vitamin and antioxidant. It is found in a variety of different fruits and vegetables, particularly citrus fruits such as oranges and lemons, but also in bell peppers, strawberries and potatoes. Some fruits and vegetables do not contain vitamin C, examples of these include bananas and cherries. The recommended daily allowance of vitamin C for adults is 60mg. A deficiency in vitamin C can lead to the disease scurvy, which causes abnormalities in the bones and gums. Vitamin C is also required for general health and can help to prevent or reduce the duration of colds. Vitamin C can be tested for by using DCPIP solution. DCPIP is pink in colour but decolourises when it comes into contact with vitamin C.

NATIONAL CURRICULUM LINKS:

Nutrition and digestion
- the content of a healthy human diet: carbohydrates, lipids (fats and oils), proteins, vitamins, minerals, dietary fibre and water, and why each is needed.

MATERIALS NEEDED:
DCPIP solution, spotting tiles, teat pipettes, selection of different fruits and vegetables to test – good choices include oranges, grapefruits, bell peppers, strawberries, bananas, potatoes, broccoli and cherries.

SAFETY AND TECHNICAL NOTES:
- It is best to use juices for this investigation. For fruit or vegetables where juices are not available, then the fruit or vegetable should be blended before the investigation.
- Very acidic substances, for example lemon juice, will cause DCPIP to not decolourise even though vitamin C is present. These substances can be diluted with water to reduce this effect.
- Be aware of any allergies and remind the students not to consume the fruit or vegetables.

METHOD:

To be done in advance by the teacher

Prepare any fruits and vegetables that need to be blended. Try to make the puree as smooth as possible. Water can be added if necessary.

STUDENTS:

1. Select the first fruit or vegetable you will be testing. Predict whether you think it will contain vitamin C.
2. Add a few drops of the fruit or vegetable juice to a spotting tile using a teat pipette.
3. Using a new teat pipette, add a few drops of the DCPIP solution to the juice in the spotting tile. If the DCPIP loses its pink colour then the fruit or vegetable contains vitamin C.
4. Repeat the investigation for the rest of the fruits and vegetables. Be sure to use a new teat pipette for each test.

DATA COLLECTION IDEAS:

Type of fruit or vegetable	Does it contain vitamin C?

DIFFERENTIATION:

- **Decrease the challenge:** The students can be given colour charts to help them decide if the DCPIP has changed colour.
- **Increase the challenge:** The students can perform a second test by boiling the fruit and vegetable juices and seeing if they obtain the same results.

USEFUL QUESTIONS TO ASK THE STUDENTS:

1. Which fruits and vegetables contained vitamin C? Were you surprised by any of your results?
2. Why is it important to have vitamin C in our diets?
3. How could we adapt the investigation to see how much vitamin C the fruits and vegetables contained?

HOMEWORK:

The students can create a healthy meal plan for one day including breakfast, lunch, dinner and snacks.

EXPERIMENT 23

Classification and identification: How can fingerprints solve a crime?

LEARNING OBJECTIVES:
Identify and classify your fingerprints.

INTRODUCTION:
The students take their own fingerprints and attempt to identify the different patterns found on them.

USEFUL PRIOR WORK:
The students should know what DNA is and its role in the body.

BACKGROUND SCIENCE:
Fingerprints are patterns on the ends of fingers caused by ridges of skin. There are different types of pattern that can be found in fingerprints, the most common ones being loops, arches and whorls. Fingerprint patterns are unique to individuals, with no two people having exactly the same fingerprints. They also never change during our lifetimes. This is useful to criminal investigators as fingerprints left behind at a crime scene can be matched to a particular individual. Fingerprints left behind at a crime scene are classified as either patent, latent or impression. Patent fingerprints are clearly visible, for example a fingerprint left in some paint. Impression prints are made in soft surfaces, for example clay or soil. Latent fingerprints are ones that are not visible but have been left on a non-porous surface, for example glass. These fingerprints can be found by 'dusting' the crime scene so they become visible and then 'lifting' them by applying a special tape over the fingerprint and transferring it onto some card.

NATIONAL CURRICULUM LINKS:

Inheritance, chromosomes, DNA and genes
- the variation between individuals within a species being continuous or discontinuous, to include measurement and graphical representation of variation.

MATERIALS NEEDED:
Washable black ink-pads, fingerprint sheets, fingerprint pattern diagrams, magnifying lenses.

SAFETY AND TECHNICAL NOTES:
- Use non-toxic inks for the fingerprinting.
- It is generally easier to take fingerprints whilst standing up.
- You may want to demonstrate the technique for taking fingerprints. The aim is to roll the fingertip from one edge of the finger to the other. The resulting print will be more of a square shape than a fingertip shape.
- The students should wash their hands after this investigation.

METHOD:

To be done in advance by the teacher
Prepare the fingerprinting sheet and fingerprint pattern diagram sheet.

STUDENTS:

1. Work in pairs to take your fingerprints.
2. Gently press your partner's first finger onto the inkpad. Try not to get too much ink onto the finger.
3. Find the correct place on the fingerprint sheet to put the print. Gently place the edge of your partner's finger onto the sheet and carefully roll it till it's flat on the paper. Continue rolling the finger until you have the entire fingerprint.
4. Repeat for the rest of the fingerprints.
5. Use a magnifying lens to examine your own fingerprints. Classify your fingerprints according to what patterns you can see on them.

DATA COLLECTION IDEAS:
Students can record their fingerprints on the fingerprinting sheet.

DIFFERENTIATION:
- **Decrease the challenge:** The students can be given assistance with taking the fingerprints.
- **Increase the challenge:** The students could also attempt to lift fingerprints from non-porous surfaces such as glass using aluminium powder and sellotape.

USEFUL QUESTIONS TO ASK THE STUDENTS:
1. What patterns did you find in your fingerprints? How did this compare to your partner?
2. Why are fingerprints useful in criminal investigations? Can you think of any limitations in using fingerprints in criminal investigations?
3. Why do you think fingerprints are left behind on certain surfaces?

HOMEWORK:
The students can research the history of fingerprints being used in criminal investigations.

EXPERIMENT 24

Classification and identification: Which plants are growing near our school?

LEARNING OBJECTIVES:
Use classification keys to identify plants growing on the school grounds.

INTRODUCTION:
The students attempt to identify plants using classification keys.

USEFUL PRIOR WORK:
The students should be able to use classification keys.

BACKGROUND SCIENCE:
All known species in the world have been named and classified by scientists. A binomial system is used where each species has its own two-part name made up of its genus and species, for example *Homo sapiens* for humans. The classification system begins with the five kingdoms (of which plants are one kingdom). The further subdivisions of kingdoms are phylum, class, order, family, genus and species. The two main classes of plants are flowering plants (angiospermae) and non-flowering plants (gymnospermae). These classes can be further sub-divided into the different species of plants. Classification keys enable us to identify different organisms quickly by providing a series of questions to follow based on the physical appearance of the organism being observed.

NATIONAL CURRICULUM LINKS:

Relationships in an ecosystem
- the interdependence of organisms in an ecosystem, including food webs and insect pollinated crops.

MATERIALS NEEDED:
A selection of classification and identification keys for plants and trees, a suitable area to carry out the investigation, magnifying lenses, data-loggers with light, pH and soil moisture sensor (optional).

SAFETY AND TECHNICAL NOTES:
- If conducting this investigation near water, ensure that the students are suitably supervised.
- Remind students not to pick any wildflowers.
- Be aware of any students who may have allergies or hay fever/asthma.
- Laminated classification and identification keys will be easier for students to use outdoors.
- The students should wash their hands after this investigation.

METHOD:

To be done in advance by the teacher
Prepare and laminate any classification keys the students will be using. These can easily be found on the Internet. You may want to survey the school grounds prior to the investigation to ensure that the students have appropriate classification and identification keys.

STUDENTS:

1. Choose a plant in the area you are surveying. Remember that trees are also a type of plant.
2. Use the classification keys you have been given to identify the plant.
3. Draw and label the plant. Use the magnifying lens to make detailed observations. Add the name if you were able to identify it correctly.
4. Use the data-logger (if you are using one) to record additional information from the area the plant is growing such as light levels and soil pH and moisture levels.
5. Repeat with other plants in the area you are surveying.

DATA COLLECTION IDEAS:

The students can produce annotated drawings of the plants they identify along with any information they gather from the data-loggers.

DIFFERENTIATION:

- **Decrease the challenge:** The students can be given a set of photographs of plants that are known to be in the area. The students then need to find where the different plants are growing.
- **Increase the challenge:** The students can collect samples of the plants they find (not wildflowers) to make additional detailed observations in the classroom.

USEFUL QUESTIONS TO ASK THE STUDENTS:

1. How challenging was it to correctly identify the plant specimens you found? Did you encounter any problems?
2. How much diversity did you discover? What might this suggest about the area we surveyed?
3. What other information could we collect to find out more about the plants we identified?

HOMEWORK:

The students can choose one plant specimen that they found and produce a detailed report on it including its classification, structure, preferred growing conditions etc.

EXPERIMENT 25

Classification and identification: What's in our food?

LEARNING OBJECTIVES:
Test different foods to see whether they contain starch, protein or fat.

INTRODUCTION:
The students will test a selection of foods and classify them based on whether they contain starch, protein and/or fat.

USEFUL PRIOR WORK:
The students should know the main food groups and what they are used for in the body.

BACKGROUND SCIENCE:
Foods are divided into five main groups based on the nutrition they contain. These food groups are carbohydrates, proteins, fats, dairy, and fruit and vegetables. A balanced diet should contain all of the five food groups in particular proportions. It is possible to test foods to see which nutrients they contain. The presence of starch, one type of carbohydrate, can be tested for using iodine. If the iodine turns black when added to a food then starch is present. Fat can be tested for using the 'grease spot' test. The food being tested can be rubbed onto a piece of filter paper. If it leaves a transparent spot on the paper then fat is present. Protein can be tested for using the Biuret test – a mixture of copper sulphate and sodium hydroxide is added to the food being tested. If the mixture turns purple then protein is present.

NATIONAL CURRICULUM LINKS:

Nutrition and digestion
- the content of a healthy human diet: carbohydrates, lipids (fats and oils), proteins, vitamins, minerals, dietary fibre and water, and why each is needed
- the consequences of imbalances in the diet, including obesity, starvation and deficiency diseases.

MATERIALS NEEDED:
Test tubes, test tube racks, teat pipettes, spotting tiles, glass rods, iodine, filter paper, cotton wool buds, Biuret solution, water, foods to test (for example, butter, milk, bread, sunflower seeds, crisps, cheese, apple).

SAFETY AND TECHNICAL NOTES:
- Eye protection should be worn for this investigation.
- Iodine is an irritant and is flammable.
- Remind the students not to consume any of the food samples.
- Be aware of any allergies.

METHOD:

To be done in advance by the teacher
Prepare the food samples to be tested. You may want to cut up larger pieces of food into smaller, roughly equal-sized pieces.

STUDENTS:

Test for carbohydrate
1 Place a small amount of each food to be tested onto a spotting tile.
2 Add a few drops of the iodine to each of the foods. If the iodine turns black then the food contains carbohydrate. Repeat for the rest of the foods.

Test for protein
1 Set up the test tubes into the test tube rack.
2 Add a small amount of each food to be tested into a test tube. If the food is a solid then add a few drops of water to the food.
3 Add a few drops of the Biuret reagent to each test tube. Shake gently. If the Biuret reagent turns purple then protein is present. Repeat for the rest of the foods.

Test for fat
1 Take a piece of filter paper and a cotton wool bud.
2 Choose the first piece of food you will be testing. If it is solid then rub a small amount directly onto the filter paper. If it is liquid or very soft then dip/rub a cotton wool bud in the food then rub this onto the filter paper.
3 Leave the filter paper to dry. If a transparent spot is left on the filter paper then fat is present. Repeat for the rest of the foods.

DATA COLLECTION IDEAS:

Type of food	Does it contain vitamin carbohydrate?	Does it contain vitamin protein?	Does it contain vitamin fat?

DIFFERENTIATION:
- **Decrease the challenge:** The students could work in small groups to test for one type of nutrient and then the results can be pooled together at the end of the investigation.
- **Increase the challenge:** The students could use ethanol for testing the presence of lipids instead of the grease spot test.

USEFUL QUESTIONS TO ASK THE STUDENTS:
1 Which foods contained carbohydrate/protein/fat? Were you surprised by any of the results?
2 What are the limitations of this investigation? How could we improve it?
3 Why is it important to eat a balanced diet?

HOMEWORK:
The students can research the other components required in a healthy diet, for example vitamins, minerals, fibre and water, and in which foods they can be found.

EXPERIMENT 26

Modelling:
Can we build a digestive system?

LEARNING OBJECTIVES:
Make a working model of the digestive system to see which substances can pass in and out of the small intestine.

INTRODUCTION:
The students use Visking tubing to make a model of the human digestive system.

USEFUL PRIOR WORK:
The students should know the main parts of the human digestive system.

BACKGROUND SCIENCE:
The digestive system is responsible for breaking down food into smaller molecules that can be used by the body in the process of respiration. Digestion begins in the mouth where food is physically broken down by the teeth and chemically broken down by the enzymes (amylase) found in saliva. The food then moves to the stomach where chemical digestion by further enzymes (protease) continues before the food moves to the small intestine. This is the final stage of digestion where the food is broken down by enzymes (amylase, protease and lipase) before it passes through the walls of the small intestine into the blood stream. Only small molecules are able to pass through the walls of the intestine so starch, which is a larger molecule, cannot pass through the wall of the intestine but glucose, (what starch is broken down into), is a small molecule so can therefore pass through the walls of the intestine.

NATIONAL CURRICULUM LINKS:

Nutrition and digestion
- the tissues and organs of the human digestive system, including adaptations to function and how the digestive system digests food (enzymes simply as biological catalysts).

MATERIALS NEEDED:
Lengths of Visking tubing – approximately 15cm long and knotted at one end, iodine solution, Benedict's reagent, 30% glucose solution, 1% starch suspension, syringes, boiling tubes, test tube racks, beakers, teat pipettes, spotting tiles, timers, cotton thread, scissors, water baths, eye protection.

SAFETY AND TECHNICAL NOTES:

- Iodine solution and Benedict's reagent are irritants.
- The water baths should be set to 90°C.
- The students should wear eye protection for this investigation.

METHOD:

To be done in advance by the teacher
Soak the lengths of Visking tubing in a beaker of water prior to the investigation in order to soften them.

STUDENTS:

1. Set up three boiling tubes in a test tube rack. These will be your model guts.
2. Add a few drops of iodine to each dimple in a spotting tile. Put this safely to one side. Fill a test tube rack with test tubes. This will be your testing rack. Put this safely to one side.
3. Use a syringe to add 10cm^3 of starch solution to a length of Visking tubing. Knot the other end of the Visking tubing and gently rinse it under water to remove any starch solution from the outside of the tubing.
4. Place the Visking tubing in one of the boiling tubes. Carefully fill the boiling tube with water and place the boiling tube back into the test tube rack.
5. Start the timer and use a teat pipette to remove a small amount of the water from the boiling tube. Place a few drops into the first dimple in the spotting tile and a few drops into the first test tube in your testing rack.
6. Remove some water from the boiling tube every minute and add it to the next dimple in your spotting tile and the next test tube in your test tube rack. Repeat this until you have five results.
7. Add a few drops of Benedict's reagent to each test tube and place the test tubes into a water bath. Leave them for a few minutes and then examine them. If they have turned orange/red then the test tube contains sugar.
8. Repeat the investigation. This time add 5cm^3 of starch solution and 5cm^3 of glucose to the Visking tubing.
9. Repeat the investigation a final time. This time add 10cm^3 of glucose to the Visking tubing.

DATA COLLECTION IDEAS:

The students can take photographs of their model guts and the resulting spotting tiles that they obtain.

DIFFERENTIATION:

- **Decrease the challenge:** The students can set up a simpler experiment with one Visking tubing containing glucose and one Visking tubing containing starch.
- **Increase the challenge:** The students can conduct the investigation at different temperatures to see if the glucose passes through the Visking tubing faster at higher temperatures.

USEFUL QUESTIONS TO ASK THE STUDENTS:

1. Which molecules were able to pass/not pass through the Visking tubing? Why do you think this was?
2. Which part of the digestive system was the Visking tubing modelling?
3. How could we model other parts of the digestive system?

HOMEWORK:

The students can find out about different types of sugars, for example sucrose, fructose, lactose, and which foods they are found in.

EXPERIMENT 27

Modelling: Can we build a DNA separating chamber?

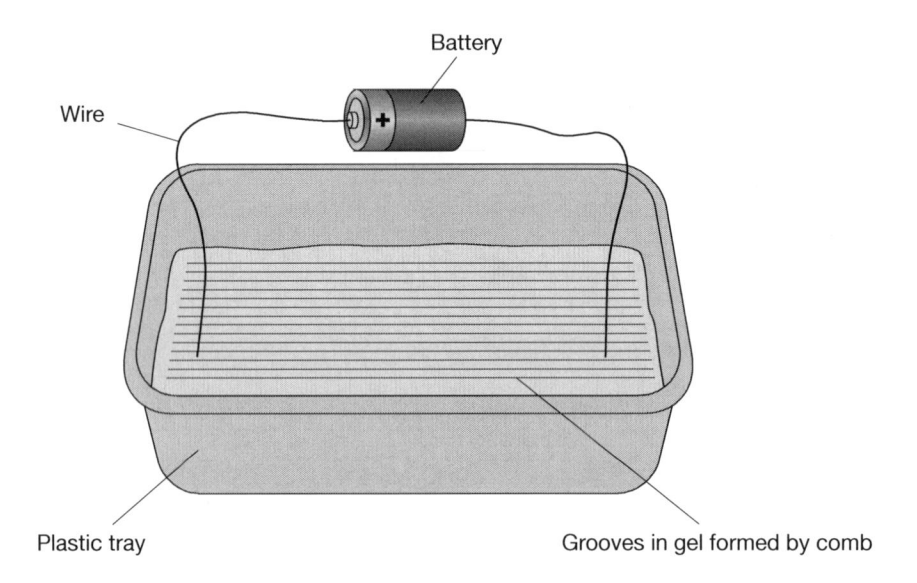

Diagram labels: Battery, Wire, Plastic tray, Grooves in gel formed by comb

LEARNING OBJECTIVES:
Build a DNA separating chamber and test it using food colouring.

INTRODUCTION:
The students build a model gel electrophoresis chamber and use the chamber to separate food colouring dyes.

USEFUL PRIOR WORK:
The students should know what DNA is and where it is found.

BACKGROUND SCIENCE:
Gel electrophoresis is a technique for separating DNA. The name comes from the use of both a gel and an electrical current during the process. The DNA sample to be separated is added to a special gel, most commonly agarose, which is made from molecules extracted from seaweed. An electrical current is then applied to the gel, causing the negatively charged nucleic acids to move away from the negatively charged end of the chamber towards the positively charged end of the chamber. As in chromatography, smaller strands of DNA are able to move further than larger strands of DNA, resulting in the separation of the different strands of DNA. The resulting separated DNA pattern could then be compared with a known sample of DNA to see if they match. This occurs in crime investigations and paternity cases.

Can we build a DNA separating chamber? 55

NATIONAL CURRICULUM LINKS:

Inheritance, chromosomes, DNA and genes
- heredity as the process by which genetic information is transmitted from one generation to the next
- a simple model of chromosomes, genes and DNA in heredity, including the part played by Watson, Crick, Wilkins and Franklin in the development of the DNA model.

MATERIALS NEEDED:
Rectangular plastic box (for example, old take-away carton), stainless steel wire, 9V batteries, battery holders, crocodile clips, scissors, measuring spoons, measuring cylinders, microwave safe bowls, plastic combs, bicarbonate of soda, agar powder, deionised water, microwave, stirrers.

⚠ SAFETY AND TECHNICAL NOTES:
- Use stainless steel wire with a gauge between 18 and 24.
- The stainless steel wire should be slightly longer than the width of the plastic trays being used.
- Use plastic combs with wide teeth.
- Supervise students when using the microwave. The bowls may become hot during the investigation.
- This investigation can be carried out over two sessions – making the separating chamber and then running the separating chamber.

METHOD:

To be done in advance by the teacher
Prepare the lengths of wire if the students will not be doing this themselves.

STUDENTS:

1. Place a piece of wire over each end of the plastic tray so that they run the width of the tray. Hook them over the edge so they stay in place. Remove the wires for now and place them somewhere safe.
2. Connect all five batteries together. Attach a crocodile clip and wire to the remaining terminals.
3. Make your buffer solution. Add 1/2 teaspoon of bicarbonate of soda to a bowl. Measure out 200ml of deionised water and add this to the bowl. Stir well.
4. Pour 100ml of the buffer solution you just made into a bowl. Add 1/2 teaspoon of agar powder to this bowl. Place the bowl in the microwave and heat for 10 seconds. Stir the contents of the bowl.
5. Keep heating the bowl for 10 seconds and stirring the contents until the mixture starts to bubble. Remove the bowl from the microwave.
6. Hold a comb up at both ends of the plastic tray. The teeth of the comb should not touch the bottom of the tray; there should be a gap of approximately 1/2 cm.
7. Carefully pour your agar mixture into the tray. Add enough mixture to just cover the bottom of the teeth of the comb.
8. Leave the tray until the agar has set (approximately 30 minutes).
9. Pour the remaining buffer solution over the solid agar in the tray.
10. Carefully pull the combs out of the tray. There should be small wells left behind which you will use for the separating part of the investigation.
11. Cut a thin slit at each end of the agar and place the wires you made earlier into them. The slits should be behind the wells you made with the comb.
12. Fill each well at one end of the agar with a different food colouring.
13. Attach the batteries to the wires in the agar. The negative end of the batteries should be attached to the wire closest to the food colouring.
14. Allow the chamber to run and check every five minutes to see the progress of the food colouring. Run until the food colouring has reached the positive electrode.

56   Can we build a DNA separating chamber?

✏ DATA COLLECTION IDEAS:
The students can take photographs of their finished DNA chambers and produce illustrated instructions on how to build one.

DIFFERENTIATION:
- **Decrease the challenge:** The DNA separating chambers can be built for the students and they can run the food colour separation.
- **Increase the challenge:** The students can compare the results from this technique with chromatography.

USEFUL QUESTIONS TO ASK THE STUDENTS:
1. What happened when the electrical current was running through the DNA chamber? Why do you think this happened?
2. Why is it useful to be able to separate DNA?
3. What are the limitations of this technique?

HOMEWORK:
The students can research the human genome project and its current applications.

EXPERIMENT 28

Modelling:
Can we build a model of DNA?

LEARNING OBJECTIVES:
Build a model strand of DNA.

INTRODUCTION:
The students use fruit and liquorice laces to build a model of DNA.

USEFUL PRIOR WORK:
The students should know what DNA is and its role in the body.

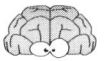

BACKGROUND SCIENCE:
All living organisms contain a molecule called DNA (deoxyribonucleic acid). In humans, this DNA is found in the nucleus of every cell. DNA contains all the genetic information for the organism. DNA is in the form of a double helix, two separate strands wrapped around each other, and is made up of smaller structures called nucleotides. Nucleotides are made up of a sugar (ribose), a phosphate group and a nitrogenous base. The nitrogenous base can be either, adenine (A), cytosine (C), guanine (G), or thymine (T). The two strands of DNA are held together by hydrogen bonds between the nitrogenous bases. However, the nitrogenous bases can only pair up in a specific way – adenine always pairs up with thymine and cytosine always pairs up with guanine. When DNA needs to replicate, the strands will unravel, exposing the nitrogenous bases, and a complementary strand of DNA will be formed along the exposed nucleotides.

NATIONAL CURRICULUM LINKS:

Genetics and evolution
- heredity as the process by which genetic information is transmitted from one generation to the next
- a simple model of chromosomes, genes and DNA in heredity, including the part played by Watson, Crick, Wilkins and Franklin in the development of the DNA model.

MATERIALS NEEDED:
Four different types of fruit, two different colours of liquorice laces, thin thread, cocktail sticks, chopping boards, knives, a worksheet with a DNA pattern for the students to follow.

SAFETY AND TECHNICAL NOTES:
- Check for any allergies before doing this investigation.
- The students should wash their hands before the investigation.
- Sterilise all surfaces before doing this investigation with a steriliser such as Milton.

METHOD:

To be done in advance by the teacher
Prepare the fruit that will be used to represent the bases. It is easier to use fruit that is a fairly uniform size such as grapes, blueberries etc. Label each type of fruit with the name of one of the four nitrogenous

bases – adenine, thymine, cytosine and guanine. Sterilise all surfaces that will be used in the investigation if the students will be allowed to eat the DNA models. Prepare a DNA pattern for the students to follow. Give the students the pattern for one strand of DNA so that they have to match the correct nitrogenous base on the other DNA strand.

STUDENTS:

1. Use the knife to cut the different coloured liquorice laces into small pieces about 2cm long. String the pieces onto the thread alternating the colours. This is the photosphate backbone of the DNA.
2. Use the pattern that you have been given to produce your model DNA. Use the cocktail sticks to attach the correct fruit 'base' to your DNA phosphate backbone. Do this until you have completed your model.
3. When you have built your model carefully lift it up and twist it around so that it forms a double helix. You have completed your DNA model.

DATA COLLECTION IDEAS:
The students can take photographs of their DNA models with annotated labels attached.

DIFFERENTIATION:
- **Decrease the challenge:** The students can build their own DNA model where they only have to match up the correct bases on each strand rather than following a pattern.
- **Increase the challenge:** The students can attempt 'DNA replication' by splitting their DNA model in half and building a complementary strand on each exposed half.

USEFUL QUESTIONS TO ASK THE STUDENTS:
1. What did each part of our model represent?
2. What do you think would happen if the wrong DNA base was added to a strand of DNA?
3. What is special about the DNA of clones?

HOMEWORK:
The students can research how DNA replicates and produce annotated diagrams.

EXPERIMENT 29

Modelling: Can we ferment our own ginger beer?

LEARNING OBJECTIVES:
Produce our own ginger beer by the process of fermentation.

INTRODUCTION:
The students make a ginger beer drink using the traditional process of fermenting yeast.

USEFUL PRIOR WORK:
The students should know what respiration is and the products of respiration.

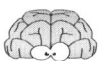

BACKGROUND SCIENCE:
Ginger beer is a low alcoholic drink made from ginger, lemon, sugar and yeast. The process of fermentation produces alcohol and carbon dioxide, making the ginger beer fizzy. Fermentation is the process of encouraging the growth of beneficial microorganisms in food in order to preserve the food and alter the taste of the food. In terms of alcohol production, the fermentation process involves the microorganism yeast. The yeast uses the sugar in the food as a food source, undergoing the process of respiration (releasing energy from food) and producing carbon dioxide gas as a waste product. When the yeast runs out of sugar it then begins the process of fermentation, producing alcohol as a waste product.

NATIONAL CURRICULUM LINKS:

Cellular respiration
- aerobic and anaerobic respiration in living organisms, including the breakdown of organic molecules to enable all the other chemical processes necessary for life
- the process of anaerobic respiration in humans and micro-organisms, including fermentation, and a word summary for anaerobic respiration
- the differences between aerobic and anaerobic respiration in terms of the reactants, the products formed and the implications for the organism.

MATERIALS NEEDED:
Chopping boards, knives, grated ginger, unwaxed lemons, cream of tartar, dried bread-making yeast, bowls, spoons, graters, sugar, balances, sieves, funnels, filter paper, steriliser (for example, Milton), empty 250ml plastic bottles.

SAFETY AND TECHNICAL NOTES:
- This investigation produces one litre of ginger beer. The students can work in groups and then decant the ginger beer into their own bottles.
- Use a steriliser such as Milton to sterilise all equipment that will be used in the investigation. Follow the directions on the packaging.

- The ginger beer produced contains a very small amount of alcohol. Some religious groups may object to the presence of any alcohol so the students should be made aware of this.
- The ginger beer should never be stored in a glass container due to the risk of explosion from the build up of carbon dioxide.
- The quantities in the investigation can be scaled up or down to produce different volumes of ginger beer.

METHOD:

To be done in advance by the teacher
Grate the ginger finely. Sterilise the plastic bottles that will be used for the ginger beer.

STUDENTS:

1. Place approximately 150g of the grated ginger into a bowl.
2. Grate the lemon over the bowl so that the rind goes into the bowl. Be careful not to grate too deeply so that the white pith does not go into the bowl.
3. Cut the lemon in half and squeeze the juice into the bowl.
4. Add 150g of sugar to the bowl and 4g of cream of tartar. Stir the contents of the bowl.
5. Add one litre of water from the hot tap to the bowl. Stir well.
6. Add 4g of yeast to the bowl and stir until you can no longer see the yeast.
7. Place some filter paper into a funnel. Place the funnel into the neck of the plastic bottle.
8. Carefully pour the ginger beer into the plastic bottle. Leave a gap of 2cm at the top of the bottle.
9. Place the lid back onto the bottle. Leave the bottle somewhere warm to ferment for 24 hours. The ginger beer will then be ready to drink. Keep the ginger beer in the fridge and drink within 5 days.

DATA COLLECTION IDEAS:
The students can produce illustrated instructions for how to make ginger beer.

DIFFERENTIATION:
- **Decrease the challenge:** The ingredients can be measured out for the students.
- **Increase the challenge:** The students can research in advance other ingredients that they could add to the ginger beer to add additional flavours.

USEFUL QUESTIONS TO ASK THE STUDENTS:
1. What caused the ginger beer to become fizzy?
2. Why is it important to make the ginger beer in a plastic rather than a glass bottle?
3. What are the advantages and disadvantages of producing ginger beer using this method?

HOMEWORK:

The students can research how other microorganisms are used in food production, for example yogurt production and soya production.

EXPERIMENT 30

Modelling:
Can we build a bug hotel?

LEARNING OBJECTIVES:
Design and build a 'bug hotel' suitable for a variety of different insects.

INTRODUCTION:
The students use a range of different materials in order to design and construct a bug hotel based on the habitats insects prefer.

USEFUL PRIOR WORK:
The students should know what conditions different insects prefer to live in.

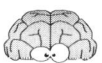

BACKGROUND SCIENCE:
Insects are essential for all life on Earth to be able to survive. They play a vital role in food chains and are responsible for pollinating certain species of plants. Despite their importance, however, many species of insects are in decline. Bees in particular are declining in number in the UK. One way to help improve the situation is to provide suitable habitats for insects. This can be done by building something called a 'bug hotel' – a structure designed to be attractive to a variety of different insects. These bug hotels will often have different mini habitats that are suitable for different insects, for example, narrow tubes for solitary bees and dark, damp areas for woodlice. The bug hotels can be placed in suitable locations outside and examined over time to see which insects have taken up residence.

NATIONAL CURRICULUM LINKS:

Relationships in an ecosystem
- the interdependence of organisms in an ecosystem, including food webs and insect pollinated crops.

MATERIALS NEEDED:
A variety of different materials for the students to construct their hotel. Good choices include: plastic drinking straws of different diameters, plastic drinks bottles, straw, dry leaves, bark, small plastic plant pots, corrugated cardboard, large stones or pebbles, bamboo canes, empty food container. Digital camera (optional).

SAFETY AND TECHNICAL NOTES:
- Make sure any items that contained food have been cleaned before being used.
- The students should wash their hands after this investigation.

METHOD:

To be done in advance by the teacher
Prepare a selection of materials for the students to use. Select a suitable place for the bug hotels to be placed if the students will not be doing this themselves.

STUDENTS:

1 Examine the materials that are available for you to build your bug hotel.
2 Make a rough sketch of the design for your hotel. Think about how you can attract different insects to the hotel.
3 Build your bug hotel. Make sure it is strong enough to survive being left outside.
4 Take a photograph of your finished bug hotel.
5 Select a suitable spot to leave your bug hotel. Come back each day to examine your bug hotel and to see which insects have taken up residence.

DATA COLLECTION IDEAS:

The students can take photographs of their bug hotel and record any bugs that they find in the hotel.

DIFFERENTIATION:

- **Decrease the challenge:** The students can be given photographs of other bug hotels to aid their designs.
- **Increase the challenge:** The students can place their bug hotel in different locations to see if that affects which bugs they observe in the hotel.

USEFUL QUESTIONS TO ASK THE STUDENTS:

1 Explain the design of your hotel. Why did you choose that design?
2 Why is it important to provide suitable habitats for insects?
3 What insects were attracted to your hotel? Why do you think this was?

HOMEWORK:

The students can find out which insects are in decline in the UK and what can be done to help improve their numbers.

EXPERIMENT 31

Modelling: Can we design and make a stethoscope?

LEARNING OBJECTIVES:
Design and build a stethoscope.

INTRODUCTION:
The students use a selection of materials to design and test different stethoscopes in order to find the best design.

USEFUL PRIOR WORK:
The students should know about the role of the heart and lungs in humans.

BACKGROUND SCIENCE:
A stethoscope is a medical instrument designed to listen to the heart and lung functions of patients. A stethoscope is a fairly simple design, consisting of ear pieces connected to a flat disk by a length of flexible plastic tubing. The disk is placed on the patient's skin, allowing the doctor to hear the patient's heart and lung sounds. The disk and tubing amplify the sounds, making them easier to hear. The stethoscope was invented in 1816 by René-Théophile-Hyacinthe Laennec. The first stethoscope consisted of a hollowed out wooden cylinder, with one end being placed on the patient's skin and the doctor placing their ear over the other end. This design was gradually refined over the years.

NATIONAL CURRICULUM LINKS:

Cells and organisation
- the hierarchical organisation of multicellular organisms: from cells to tissues to organs to systems to organisms.

Gas exchange systems
- the structure and functions of the gas exchange system in humans, including adaptations to function
- the mechanism of breathing to move air in and out of the lungs, using a pressure model to explain the movement of gases, including simple measurements of lung volume.

MATERIALS NEEDED:
Plastic tubing of different lengths, cardboard tubes of different lengths, funnels of different sizes, drinking straws, sellotape, scissors.

SAFETY AND TECHNICAL NOTES:
- Use non-bendy drinking straws for this investigation.

METHOD:

To be done in advance by the teacher
Prepare a selection of materials for the students to use to make their stethoscope.

64 *Can we design and make a stethoscope?*

STUDENTS:

1 Examine the materials you have been given. Sketch a rough design for three different stethoscopes that you can make using these materials.
2 Build your first stethoscope. Test it by placing the stethoscope on your partner's back. Listen to the sounds you can hear. Place the stethoscope in different places on your partner's back. Can you hear their heart beat? Can you hear any breathing sounds?
3 Build your second and third stethoscopes and test them in the same way. Decide which is the best stethoscope. Why do you think that design worked well?

DATA COLLECTION IDEAS:
The students can take photographs of their finished stethoscopes and produce illustrated instructions for how to make one.

DIFFERENTIATION:
- **Decrease the challenge:** The students can be given instructions on how to make three different stethoscopes, which they can then build and test.
- **Increase the challenge:** The students can conduct a more systematic, fair-test style investigation for comparing the stethoscopes.

USEFUL QUESTIONS TO ASK THE STUDENTS:
1 What was the best design for the stethoscope? Why do you think this was?
2 How could the design for your stethoscope be improved?
3 Why is the stethoscope an important piece of medical equipment?

HOMEWORK:
The students can research the history and development of the stethoscope.

EXPERIMENT 32

Observation:
Can a solid turn into a gas?

LEARNING OBJECTIVES:
Observe whether a solid can change state directly to a gas.

INTRODUCTION:
The students use a water bath to heat a solid air freshener in order to observe sublimation.

USEFUL PRIOR WORK:
The students should know the particle theory of matter.

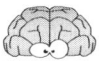

BACKGROUND SCIENCE:
Sublimation is a physical change of state whereby a solid changes to a gas without passing through the liquid state. This occurs because the substance takes on so much energy so quickly that melting does not take place. Sublimation occurs at temperatures and pressures below a substance's triple point (the point at which it can exist in all three states of matter – solid, liquid and gas). Different substances will undergo sublimation at different temperatures. Dry ice and solid carbon dioxide are examples of substances that can undergo sublimation. Solid air fresheners can also undergo sublimation at temperatures over 45°C. The opposite of sublimation (when a gas changes state to a solid without passing through the liquid state) is called de-sublimation or deposition.

NATIONAL CURRICULUM LINKS:

The particulate nature of matter
- the properties of the different states of matter (solid, liquid and gas) in terms of the particle model, including gas pressure
- changes of state in terms of the particle model.

Physical changes
- conservation of material and of mass, and reversibility, in melting, freezing, evaporation, sublimation, condensation, dissolving.

MATERIALS NEEDED:
Beakers, thermometers, shallow dishes, boss and clamp stand, solid air freshener broken into small pieces, cubes of ice, hot water, fume cupboard, eye protection.

SAFETY AND TECHNICAL NOTES:
- This investigation needs to be carried out in a fume cupboard as a demonstration.
- Used coloured air fresheners if possible. This will help to demonstrate that the air freshener sublimes but the dye does not.
- Eye protection should be worn for this investigation.
- The hot water used must be at least 45°C.
- The investigation can take a few minutes to conduct.

66   *Can a solid turn into a gas?*

METHOD:

To be done in advance by the teacher
Break up the solid air freshener into small pieces.

STUDENTS:

1 Place the pieces of solid air freshener into a beaker. Place this beaker onto a shallow dish in a fume cupboard.
2 Fill another beaker 3/4 of the way with the cubed iced. Use the boss and clamp stand to place this beaker directly over the beaker containing the air freshener. The bottom of the beaker should touch the top of the beaker containing the air freshener.
3 Fill the shallow dish with hot water. Observe what happens to the solid.

DATA COLLECTION IDEAS:
The students can draw a diagram of the equipment used and what happens in the investigation.

DIFFERENTIATION:
- **Decrease the challenge:** Recording the sublimation process and playing it back for the students may allow them more opportunity to observe what is happening.
- **Increase the challenge:** The students can observe the sublimation of more than one substance to see if there are any similarities or differences.

USEFUL QUESTIONS TO ASK THE STUDENTS:
1 What did you observe happening to the air freshener? Why do you think this happened?
2 What do you think might have happened if we had used a temperature lower than 45°C? Why do you think this?
3 How can sublimation be useful to us in everyday life?

HOMEWORK:
The students can research the use of dry ice in theatre productions including how it works and its effects.

EXPERIMENT 33

Observation:
Where should we dig for oil?

LEARNING OBJECTIVES:
Observe different types of sedimentary rocks to see which ones are most likely to store oil.

INTRODUCTION:
The students carry out detailed observations of sedimentary rocks including whether they are able to absorb oil.

USEFUL PRIOR WORK:
The students should know about the three main types of rocks.

BACKGROUND SCIENCE:
Oil is an example of a fossil fuel (the other two being coal and gas) that is found in the ground between layers of rock. Oil is extracted from the ground by digging a well down into the oil and then pumping out the oil. As well as being used as a fuel to produce electricity, oil can also be refined (broken down) into other useful products including petrol for cars, kerosene fuel for aeroplanes, certain types of plastic and tarmac for road. This makes oil a very useful and valuable product. A problem with oil is that we do not always know where it can be found. One way that scientists can locate oil is to study the types of rock in a particular area. Oil will often form where there are sedimentary rocks present. A reservoir rock is a sedimentary rock that is permeable and porous and will allow oil to pass through it whereas a cap rock is a sedimentary rock that is not permeable to oil. Oil will pass up through the reservoir rock but will be stopped from moving any higher by the cap rock. The oil will then remain stored in the reservoir rock.

NATIONAL CURRICULUM LINKS:

Earth and atmosphere
- the rock cycle and the formation of igneous, sedimentary and metamorphic rocks
- Earth as a source of limited resources and the efficacy of recycling.

MATERIALS NEEDED:
A selection of sedimentary rocks, for example, limestone, sandstone, chalk, shale, conglomerate, oil (for example, cooking oil), magnifying lenses, teat-pipettes, timers.

SAFETY AND TECHNICAL NOTES:
- Use rock samples that are a similar size.

METHOD:

To be done in advance by the teacher
Prepare and label the sedimentary rocks that will be used by the students.

STUDENTS:

1. Observe the different sedimentary rocks you have been given in detail using your magnifying lens. What does the rock look and feel like? Record your observations.
2. Place the different rocks onto a white tile. Add a few drops of oil to each rock using the teat-pipette. Record what you observe.
3. Leave the rocks for 20 minutes then come back and examine them again. What has happened to the oil? Use the magnifying lens to make detailed observations.
4. From your observations, decide which rocks would be reservoir rocks and which would be cap rocks.

DATA COLLECTION IDEAS:

Type of rock	Observations

DIFFERENTIATION:

- **Decrease the challenge:** The students can compare a known cap rock with a known reservoir rock and observe the differences when oil is added to them.
- **Increase the challenge:** The students can carry out further observations of the rocks including their density and volume.

USEFUL QUESTIONS TO ASK THE STUDENTS:

1. What similarities and differences were there between the different sedimentary rocks?
2. Which rocks do you think are reservoir/cap rocks? Were you surprised by any of your results?
3. How would this information be helpful to scientists who are looking for oil?

HOMEWORK:

The students can research the different uses of refined oil.

EXPERIMENT 34

Observation: What colour are M&Ms?

LEARNING OBJECTIVES:
Determine which colours are in M&Ms by carrying out chromatography.

INTRODUCTION:
The students use paper chromatography to correctly identify which colours are found in the coloured shells of M&Ms.

USEFUL PRIOR WORK:
The students should know that some substances can be separated.

BACKGROUND SCIENCE:
Chromatography is a technique used to separate mixtures or solutions. There are different kinds of chromatography, one of which is paper chromatography. In paper chromatography a small amount of a coloured solution or mixture is added to the end of a strip of chromatography paper. The paper is then placed into a liquid that will then pass up the paper and carry the solution or mixture with it. The mixture or solution will contain different components that will be separated out as the liquid travels up the paper. The components are separated as they are different sizes, with heavier components travelling a shorter distance than lighter components. This investigation works better with M&Ms rather than Smarties as they contain artificial dyes.

NATIONAL CURRICULUM LINKS:

Pure and impure substances
- mixtures, including dissolving
- simple techniques for separating mixtures: filtration, evaporation, distillation and chromatography.

MATERIALS NEEDED:
Chromatography paper or filter paper strips, splints, beakers, teat-pipettes, paintbrushes, pencils, paper towels, M&Ms.

SAFETY AND TECHNICAL NOTES:
- M&Ms work better for this investigation than Smarties.
- Remind the students not to consume the M&Ms unless they have permission. Check if the M&Ms are suitable for vegetarians.
- Be aware of any allergies.

METHOD:

To be done in advance by the teacher
Separate the M&Ms into their different colours.

What colour are M&Ms?

STUDENTS:

1. Fill a beaker with water. Select the first M&M you will be testing and place it on a paper towel.
2. Draw a pencil line along the bottom of your chromatography paper about 1cm from the bottom of the paper.
3. Use the teat-pipette to add a few drops of water to the M&M. Don't make it too wet; you just want to release some of the dye.
4. Use the paintbrush to transfer the dye from the M&M to the pencil line on your chromatography paper. You want to make a concentrated dot in the middle of the line.
5. Add a small amount of water to a beaker. Fold the top end of your chromatography paper over a wooden splint. It should be able to hang down without falling off the splint.
6. Place the splint into the beaker so that the chromatography paper touches the water in the beaker. It should only just touch the water.
7. Leave the beaker until the water has travelled to the top of the chromatography paper. Remove and place the chromatography paper onto a paper towel to dry. Record what colours you can see.
8. Repeat for the other M&Ms.

DATA COLLECTION IDEAS:

Colour of M&M	Colours found in the dye

DIFFERENTIATION:

- **Decrease the challenge:** The students can perform a simpler form of paper chromatography by placing the coloured dot in the middle of a round piece of filter paper and adding a few drops of water to the dot.
- **Increase the challenge:** The students can calculate the relative front factor for each separated colour using the equation: R_f = Distance travelled by component/distance travelled by solvent.

USEFUL QUESTIONS TO ASK THE STUDENTS:

1. What colours did you find in the M&Ms? Were you surprised by any of your results?
2. Do you think you would obtain the same results if you used a different test subject, for example coloured pens?
3. Where in everyday life would chromatography be useful?

HOMEWORK:

The students can research how chromatography is used at crime scenes.

EXPERIMENT 35

Observation: What is the best material for a campfire?

LEARNING OBJECTIVES:
Observe how different materials burn in order to choose the best material to make a campfire.

INTRODUCTION:
The students use a Bunsen burner to set different materials alight in order to see how they burn and how much energy they release.

USEFUL PRIOR WORK:
The students should know the fire triangle.

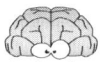

BACKGROUND SCIENCE:
A fuel is a substance that can undergo the chemical reaction of combustion. Combustion occurs if a fuel is heated to a high enough temperature that its ignition point is reached whilst it is in the presence of oxygen. The visible results of combustion are flames or a glow. The process of combustion produces energy in the form of heat and light. There are two types of combustion: complete combustion – which occurs if there is a plentiful supply of oxygen present, and incomplete combustion – which occurs if there is a limited supply of oxygen. The products of complete combustion are carbon dioxide and water. Incomplete combustion produces some carbon and carbon monoxide alongside carbon dioxide and water. Complete combustion is also more efficient than incomplete combustion and will produce more energy.

NATIONAL CURRICULUM LINKS:

Chemical reactions
- combustion, thermal decomposition, oxidation and displacement reactions.

MATERIALS NEEDED:
Bunsen burners, safety mats, eye protection, tongs, timers, materials for the students to use, for example: wooden splints, newspaper, charcoal, tissue paper, thick string, cotton wool.

SAFETY AND TECHNICAL NOTES:
- Demonstrate to the students how to burn items safely and how to extinguish the material safely if needed.
- Only provide materials that are safe to burn in the classroom and will not produce any toxic fumes.

METHOD:

To be done in advance by the teacher
Have a selection of materials for the student to use. Try to make the different pieces roughly the same size – a few centimetres long will be sufficient.

72 What is the best material for a campfire?

STUDENTS:

1. Set up a boss and clamp stand. Half fill a boiling tube with water and place it in the clamp. The boiling tube should be angled at about 45°. Lower the boiling tube so that it is about half way down the clamp stand.
2. Set up a Bunsen burner near your clamp stand and place it on the yellow flame.
3. Select the first fuel you want to test. Use a balance to measure the mass of the fuel. Record this in your table. Observe the fuel closely before it is burnt and record your observations in your table.
4. Use a thermometer to take the temperature of the water in the boiling tube. Record this in your table.
5. Use the Bunsen burner to light the fuel. Hold it in the flame of the Bunsen burner until you can see that it has caught alight. Carefully place the burning fuel directly underneath the boiling tube. The flame does not have to touch the boiling tube. Observe what happens as the fuel burns. Record your observations.
6. When the fuel has stopped burning take the temperature of the water again. Record this in your table. Observe what is left of the fuel and record this in your table.
7. Repeat for the other fuels.

DATA COLLECTION IDEAS:

Type of material	Mass of material (g)	Temp. of water at start (°C)	Temp. of water at end (°C)	Observations

DIFFERENTIATION:
- **Decrease the challenge:** The students can simply observe what happens when the materials are burnt and make qualitative observations.
- **Increase the challenge:** The students can use a more accurate calorimeter for the investigation.

USEFUL QUESTIONS TO ASK THE STUDENTS:
1. Which material would be the best/worst material to use for a campfire? What evidence do you have for this decision?
2. Apart from how well it burns, what other factors would affect how good a material is for using in a campfire?
3. What are the risks of having a fire outdoors? How could these risks be minimised?

HOMEWORK:
The students could research forest fires including the countries they are prevalent in, the damage caused and how they are dealt with.

EXPERIMENT 36

Observation:
How can we make colourful flames?

LEARNING OBJECTIVES:
Observe the different coloured flames produced when solutions of metal salts are burnt

INTRODUCTION:
The students perform flame tests using a number of different metal salt solutions in order to see the colour of the flame produced.

USEFUL PRIOR WORK:
The students should be able to use a Bunsen burner.

BACKGROUND SCIENCE:
This investigation involves burning metal salt solutions in the flame of a Bunsen burner. If a metal salt solution is introduced to a naked flame then the electrons in the metal gain energy. This energy allows them to jump from their current electron shell to a higher electron shell. However, the electron is unable to stay in this electron shell and will return to its original electron shell, giving off energy in the form of light as it does so. This will make the flame appear to change colour. The colour will depend on which metal is contained in the metal salt solution. Calcium gives an orange flame, copper (II) a blue or green flame, potassium a lilac flame, barium a pale green flame, lithium a red flame and sodium a yellow flame. These metal salts are often used in fireworks in order to produce the different colours.

NATIONAL CURRICULUM LINKS:

Chemical reactions
- combustion, thermal decomposition, oxidation and displacement reactions.

MATERIALS NEEDED:
Bunsen burners, safety mats, test tube racks, flame test wires, eye protection, hydrochloric acid, 0.5M solutions of barium chloride, calcium chloride, copper (II) sulphate, lead (II) sulphate, potassium nitrate and sodium chloride.

SAFETY AND TECHNICAL NOTES:
- The students should wear eye protection for this investigation.
- Hydrochloric acid is an irritant.
- It is best for students to conduct the sodium test last as it is hard to remove all traces of sodium from the flame test wire.

METHOD:

To be done in advance by the teacher
Prepare three 'unknown samples' of metal salt solutions for the students to test and identify after the flame tests.

74   How can we make colourful flames?

STUDENTS:

1. Set up a Bunsen burner and set it on the safety flame until you need to use it.
2. Take your flame test wire and dip it into the hydrochloric acid.
3. Put your Bunsen burner onto the blue flame and hold the flame test wire in the hottest part of the flame. If you see no colour change then the wire is clean. If you see a colour change then repeat dipping the wire into the hydrochloric acid and burning the wire in the flame until you see no colour change.
4. Dip the flame test wire into one of the known metal salt solutions. Hold the flame test wire in the hottest part of the flame.
5. Observe the colour change of the flame and record this in your results table.
6. Repeat for the rest of the known metal salt solutions. Make sure you clean your flame test wire between the different metal salt solutions by dipping the wire into the hydrochloric acid and holding the wire in the hottest part of the flame.
7. When you have completed all the known samples you now need to test the unknown samples. Test each sample and see if you can identify which metal salt solution it contains. Remember to clean the flame test wire between samples.

DATA COLLECTION IDEAS:

Metal salt	Colour of flame

DIFFERENTIATION:
- **Decrease the challenge:** The students can be given a separate flame test wire for each metal salt solution they are testing in order to prevent cross-contamination.
- **Increase the challenge:** The students can see what happens to the colour of the flame when more than one metal salt solution is present.

USEFUL QUESTIONS TO ASK THE STUDENTS:
1. What did you observe when the metal salt solutions were burnt?
2. Why do you think the flames turned different colours when the metal salt solutions were burnt?
3. Where would this be useful in everyday life?

HOMEWORK:
The students can research the history of fireworks and how the materials they are made from have developed over time.

EXPERIMENT 37

Observation:
What is special about the melting and freezing point of a substance?

LEARNING OBJECTIVES:
Observe the melting and freezing points of stearic acid and plot the resulting melting and cooling curve.

INTRODUCTION:
The students use a Bunsen burner to melt solid stearic acid and record the changes of temperature before allowing the stearic acid to cool and solidify again.

USEFUL PRIOR WORK:
The students should understand the terms melting and freezing point.

BACKGROUND SCIENCE:
Melting and freezing are examples of physical changes of state. The melting point of a substance is the temperature at which a solid becomes a liquid at normal atmospheric pressure. The freezing point of a substance is the temperature at which a liquid becomes a solid at normal atmospheric pressure. Theoretically, the melting point and the freezing point of a substance should be the same. A solid will melt if it is exposed to energy in the form of heat. This energy will provide the particles that make up the solid with more energy that will allow them to vibrate with greater energy, eventually breaking the intermolecular forces holding the particles together. The particles are then able to move freely and the solid will turn into a liquid. Different substances have different melting and freezing points. Stearic acid has a melting point of around 55–70°C depending on the purity of the substance (the purer the substance the higher the melting point).

NATIONAL CURRICULUM LINKS:

The particulate nature of matter
- the properties of the different states of matter (solid, liquid and gas) in terms of the particle model, including gas pressure
- changes of state in terms of the particle model.

Atoms, elements and compounds
- conservation of mass changes of state and chemical reactions.

Energetics
- energy changes on changes of state (qualitative).

MATERIALS NEEDED:
Bunsen burners, tripods, gauze, heat-proof mats, beakers, thermometers, stirring rods, boiling tubes, timers, eye protection, stearic acid, tongs, test tube rack, data-loggers (optional).

SAFETY AND TECHNICAL NOTES:
- Eye protection should be worn for this investigation.

76 Melting and freezing point of a substance

- The water does not need to be boiling continuously for this investigation. The students can move the Bunsen burner from underneath the beaker when the water has started boiling vigorously and return it when the water has stopped bubbling.
- The stearic acid can be re-used after the investigation.
- Data-loggers can be used instead of thermometers for this investigation.

METHOD:

To be done in advance by the teacher
Add about 10g of solid stearic acid to the boiling tubes.

STUDENTS:

1 Set up a Bunsen burner with a tripod, gauze and heatproof mat.
2 Add 150ml of water to a beaker. Place the beaker onto the gauze. Heat the water until it is boiling.
3 When the water is boiling you can move the Bunsen burner away from the beaker. Your aim is to try to keep the water at a reasonably constant temperature. If the water stops bubbling put the Bunsen burner back under the beaker until the water is boiling again.
4 Place a boiling tube containing the stearic acid into the beaker. Put a thermometer and stirring rod into the boiling tube. Stir the stearic acid using the stirring rod throughout the experiment.
5 Record the temperature of the stearic acid every minute until no more solid remains. Record the time at which you first saw the solid change into a liquid.
6 Use the tongs to remove the boiling tube from the beaker of water. Place it into a test tube rack. Record the temperature of the stearic acid every minute until no more liquid remains. Remember to keep stirring the stearic acid for as long as you can. Record the time at which you first saw the liquid change into a solid.

DATA COLLECTION IDEAS:

Time (m)	Temp. of stearic acid (°C)

DIFFERENTIATION:

- **Decrease the challenge:** The students might find it easier to use a data-logger rather than a thermometer for this investigation. The data-logger could be set up with a computer so that the results are plotted onto a graph for the students.
- **Increase the challenge:** The students can compare stirring with non-stirring to see the effect this has on the melting and freezing point.

USEFUL QUESTIONS TO ASK THE STUDENTS:

1 What did you observe about the melting and freezing points of the stearic acid?
2 Why do you think we stirred the stearic acid during the experiment?
3 What do you think would happen if we used stearic acid that contained a lot of impurities?

HOMEWORK:

The students can produce a graph of their results.

EXPERIMENT 38

Fair testing: Which is the best washing powder?

LEARNING OBJECTIVES:
Investigate whether biological washing powders are better at removing stains than non-biological washing powders.

INTRODUCTION:
The students compare how effective biological and non-biological washing powders are at removing different types of stain from cloth.

USEFUL PRIOR WORK:
The students should know what enzymes are.

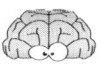

BACKGROUND SCIENCE:
Washing powders generally fall into two categories: biological and non-biological. Biological washing powders contain enzymes (a biological catalyst), whereas non-biological washing powders do not contain enzymes. Biological washing powders are usually thought of as being better at removing biological stains from clothing, for example grass stains, due to the presence of these enzymes. Some possible disadvantages of using biological washing powders are: some people can have allergic reactions to the trace amounts of enzymes left behind on clothing, the need to use a lower water temperature for washing the clothes in order to not break down the enzymes and the possibility of enzymes damaging natural fabrics such as wool and silk.

NATIONAL CURRICULUM LINKS:

Chemical reactions
- what catalysts do.

MATERIALS NEEDED:
Small pieces of white cotton fabric, substances to make stains (for example, felt pen, grass, chocolate, oil-based paint, nail varnish, egg), biological washing powder, non-biological washing powder, beakers, measuring spoons, timers, non-latex gloves, paper towels.

SAFETY AND TECHNICAL NOTES:
- Use powder-based washing powders for this investigation.
- Stains should be approximately the size of a 10 pence coin.
- The students should wear gloves for this investigation.
- Be aware of any allergies.
- Water from the hot tap will be sufficient for this investigation.

METHOD:

To be done in advance by the teacher
Cut the fabric into small, roughly even-sized squares. Approximately 3cm × 3cm will be sufficient.

STUDENTS:

1 Prepare the stains that you will be using for your investigation. Place one type of stain in the middle of each piece of fabric. Try to make your stains roughly the same size.
2 Set up one beaker for each piece of fabric. Fill each beaker with water from the hot tap.
3 Add one teaspoon of the biological washing powder to each beaker and stir a few times to help dissolve the powder.
4 Add the pieces of fabric to the beakers. Stir a few times then start the timer. Leave the fabric in the beaker for 10 minutes. Whilst you are waiting, make the next set of stains for the investigation and set up the beakers for the non-biological washing powder.
5 When the 10 minutes have passed, remove each piece of fabric from the beaker and rinse it for a few seconds under the cold tap. Place them on some paper towels to dry.
6 Repeat the investigation for the non-biological washing powder. When you have finished, compare the results for the two types of powder.

DATA COLLECTION IDEAS:

The students can take photographs of their fabric samples before and after the investigation and/or measure the size of the stain before and after the investigation.

DIFFERENTIATION:

- **Decrease the challenge:** The students can investigate just two stains, one biological and one non-biological.
- **Increase the challenge:** The students can work in groups in order to investigate other factors, for example, temperature of water or agitation of water, and the results can be pooled at the end of the investigation.

USEFUL QUESTIONS TO ASK THE STUDENTS:

1 Which type of powder was best at removing biological/non-biological stains? Why do you think this was?
2 What are the advantages and disadvantages of using washing powders that contain enzymes?
3 How could we improve this investigation?

HOMEWORK:

The students can research alternative methods for cleaning clothes, such as soap flakes and borax, including how they work.

EXPERIMENT 39

Fair testing:
Can we prevent rusting?

LEARNING OBJECTIVES:
Investigate how rusting occurs and whether it can be prevented.

INTRODUCTION:
The students investigate the conditions that are required for rusting to occur and different ways to prevent rusting by using nails left in different conditions.

USEFUL PRIOR WORK:
The students should know what rust is and that it can cause damage to metal structures.

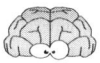

BACKGROUND SCIENCE:
Rusting, also known as corrosion, affects the metals iron and steel (steel is an alloy of iron, which means it contains iron). Rust is actually deposits of iron oxide formed when iron reacts with oxygen in the air. Water is also needed for rusting to occur. Rusting is an example of a non-reversible chemical change as a new product is being formed (iron oxide) and it is not possible to reverse the change and release the iron and oxygen. Rusting is not desirable as it can cause irreparable damage to metal, both structurally and cosmetically. Rusting can be prevented by stopping either oxygen or water from coming into contact with the metal. This typically involves the use of a physical barrier such as a paint or grease. It can also be prevented by the process of galvanisation, where iron or steel is covered in a thin layer of zinc.

NATIONAL CURRICULUM LINKS:

Chemical reactions
- combustion, thermal decomposition, oxidation and displacement reaction.

Materials
- the order of metals and carbon in the reactivity series.

MATERIALS NEEDED:
Iron nails, painted iron nails, boiling tubes, test tube rack, cooking oil, grease such as petroleum jelly, anhydrous calcium chloride, spatulas, water.

SAFETY AND TECHNICAL NOTES:
- Anhydrous calcium chloride is an irritant.
- For the investigation with boiled water and cooking oil, the water should be added to the beaker first and then a thin layer of cooking oil should be poured on top of the water. This prevents oxygen from entering the boiled water.
- The nails should ideally be left for a week.

80 *Can we prevent rusting?*

METHOD:

To be done in advance by the teacher
Paint the required number of nails and ensure they have time to dry fully before starting the investigation. Boil the water that will be used for the investigation and allow it to cool.

STUDENTS:

1. Place five boiling tubes in a test tube rack.
2. Add a nail to one boiling tube. Fill the boiling tube with water so that the nail is completely covered.
3. Add a nail to one boiling tube. Fill the boiling tube with water so that the nail is completely covered. Carefully pour cooking oil on top of the water so that it forms a thin layer. The oil prevents oxygen from entering the water.
4. Add a nail to one boiling tube. Use a spatula to add anhydrous calcium chloride to the boiling tube. Add enough anhydrous calcium chloride so that the bottom half of the nail is covered. The anhydrous calcium chloride prevents water from entering the boiling tube.
5. Add a painted nail to one boiling tube. Fill the boiling tube with water so that the nail is completely covered.
6. Cover a nail with grease such as petroleum jelly. Add the nail to a boiling tube. Fill the boiling tube with water so that the nail is completely covered.

DATA COLLECTION IDEAS:

Type of nail	Observations

DIFFERENTIATION:

- **Decrease the challenge:** The students can work in small groups, with one group investigating one condition. The results can then be pooled at the end of the investigation.
- **Increase the challenge:** The students can compare the effects of different types of water on rusting, for example deionised water, mineral water, tap water etc.

USEFUL QUESTIONS TO ASK THE STUDENTS:
1. In which conditions did rusting occur/not occur? Why do you think this happened?
2. What can you observe about the nails where rusting has occurred?
3. Why is rusting damaging to iron and steel structures?

HOMEWORK:
The students can research how 'rusticles' form underwater on, for example, shipwrecks.

EXPERIMENT 40

Fair testing:
Which antacid is the most effective?

LEARNING OBJECTIVES:
Investigate which is the best antacid for neutralising excess stomach acid.

INTRODUCTION:
The students compare the effects of different antacids on a sample of 'stomach acid' to determine which is the most effective medication.

USEFUL PRIOR WORK:
Students should know what acids and alkalis are and how neutralisation occurs.

BACKGROUND SCIENCE:
The human stomach produces hydrochloric acid for a number of reasons, the main reason being that pepsin, the enzyme that breaks down proteins in the stomach, works best under acidic conditions. The acid in the stomach also helps to prevent infection by destroying microorganisms that may have been ingested. The pH of the acid in the stomach is typically around pH2. Normally, the acid in the stomach does not cause us any problems. Occasionally, however, too much acid can be produced in the stomach, which can lead to acid reflux or 'heartburn'. This is where acid from the stomach flows up into the oesophagus (gullet) and causes a burning sensation in the back of the throat. Antacids are alkali compounds; they usually contain aluminium, calcium or magnesium. Antacids can work in one of two ways – they can neutralise the excess stomach acid or they can form a layer on top of the acid to prevent it from flowing up into the oesophagus. Antacids are a short-term cure for temporary excessive stomach acid and should not be used on a long-term basis.

NATIONAL CURRICULUM LINKS:

Chemical reactions
- defining acids and alkalis in terms of neutralisation reactions
- the pH scale for measuring acidity/alkalinity; and indicators
- reactions of acids with alkalis to produce a salt plus water.

Nutrition and digestion
- The tissues and organs of the human digestive system, including adaptations to function and how the digestive system digests food (enzymes simply as biological catalysts).

MATERIALS NEEDED:
Hydrochloric acid, three different types of antacid medication, ideally one in powder form, one in tablet form and one in liquid form, measuring cylinders, pestle and mortars, beakers, spatulas, timers, universal indicator or data-logger with pH sensor, labels, eye protection.

SAFETY AND TECHNICAL NOTES:
- The students should wear eye protection for this investigation.
- Hydrochloric acid and universal indicator are irritants.
- Retain all the packaging for the antacid medications for the students to use during the investigation.

Which antacid is the most effective?

- If using antacid tablets – the students should use the pestle and mortar to grind these up before using them in the investigation. This is because most antacid tablets need to be chewed before swallowing.
- Have students set up a 'control stomach' that they can compare with the test stomachs. If they are using universal indicator it will make it easier for them to see the changes in the colour of the indicator.

METHOD:

To be done in advance by the teacher
Have the packaging for the different types of antacid available for the students to use.

STUDENTS:

1. Prepare your 'stomachs' for testing. Measure 50ml of the hydrochloric acid and add this to a beaker. Label this beaker 'control stomach'. Add universal indicator to this beaker or use the data-logger to measure the pH of the stomach acid.
2. Measure 50ml of the hydrochloric acid and add this to another beaker. Label this beaker with the name of the first antacid medication you will be testing. If you are using universal indicator then add this to the beaker as well.
3. Look at the packaging the antacid came in to see what a normal dose of the medication is. Measure out the normal dose of the antacid. If the antacid is a tablet then use the pestle and mortar to crush up the tablets.
4. Add the antacid to the beaker. Start the stopcock and time for one minute.
5. Observe what happens in the beaker and write down your observations.
6. Record the pH of the stomach acid using the colour of the universal indicator or the data-logger.
7. Repeat the investigation two more times for that antacid. Calculate the average pH achieved after one minute.
8. Repeat the experiment for the other two antacid medications.

DATA COLLECTION IDEAS:

Type of antacid	pH of stomach acid after one minute				Observations
	Trial 1	Trial 2	Trial 3	Average	

DIFFERENTIATION:

- **Decrease the challenge:** The students could add the antacid medication to the acid until the neutral point is reached and calculate how much of the medication (i.e. how many tablets) was needed to reach the neutral point.
- **Increase the challenge:** The students could consider other factors regarding the antacids, for example they could calculate the cost of each individual 'dose' of the antacid by using the cost of the antacid and by working out how many doses there are in a packet.

USEFUL QUESTIONS TO ASK THE STUDENTS:
1 Which antacid do you think is the most effective? Why do you think this?
2 What did you observe when you added the antacid to the stomach acid? Why do you think this happened?
3 What other factors would you consider when choosing an antacid?

HOMEWORK:
The students could research the causes and possible complications of excess stomach acid, including long-term medication options for people with frequent excess stomach acid.

EXPERIMENT 41

Fair testing: Which is the best brand of disposable nappies?

LEARNING OBJECTIVES:
Investigate whether expensive, branded nappies are better than cheaper, shop brand nappies.

INTRODUCTION:
The students compare the effectiveness of different brands of disposable nappies by comparing how much water they can absorb.

USEFUL PRIOR WORK:
The students should understand the term volume.

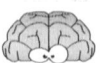

BACKGROUND SCIENCE:
A hydrogel is an example of a smart material (they are referred to as smart materials as they are able to change their shape due to a change in their environment). Hydrogels are polymers that are able to absorb many times their own weight in water. They are able to do this because they are polymers formed from carboxylic acids that will ionise when they come into contact with water. This causes negative charges to occur along the polymers, forcing the polymer to expand (as the negative charges will repel each other) and attracting the polar charged water molecules. This allows the hydrogel to absorb the water. Hydrogels are found in many everyday products such as disposable nappies and hair gel.

NATIONAL CURRICULUM LINKS:

Atoms, elements and compounds
- conservation of mass changes of state and chemical reactions.

MATERIALS NEEDED:
A selection of different disposable nappies including, for example, branded nappies such as Pampers, shop's own brand nappies and eco-friendly nappies, scissors, plastic trays or large tubs, measuring spoons, beakers, stirring rods, distilled water, eye protection, non-latex gloves.

SAFETY AND TECHNICAL NOTES:
- Eye protection and gloves should be worn for this investigation.

METHOD:

To be done in advance by the teacher
Keep the packaging from the nappies for the students to examine.

STUDENTS:

1. Select the first disposable nappy you will be testing. Cut out the middle section that is designed to absorb the urine.

2 Place the section you have cut out into a large tub or tray. Make sure the tub or tray is completely dry.
3 Gently pull apart the nappy section you have cut out. White grains will fall out of the nappy. Collect as much of the white material as you can. Do this part very gently as the material is very light and can easily be blown away.
4 Use a spoon to carefully transfer the white grains to a beaker. Use the beaker to estimate the volume of the white grains. Record this in your table.
5 Add 100ml of distilled water to the beaker and stir. Keep adding distilled water until no more can be absorbed. Record the volume of water added in your results table.
6 Repeat the investigation with the rest of the nappies.

DATA COLLECTION IDEAS:

Brand of nappy	Estimated vol. of water absorbing grains in nappy	Vol. of water grains absorbed (ml)

DIFFERENTIATION:
- **Decrease the challenge:** The students may need help collecting the hydrogel from the nappy.
- **Increase the challenge:** The students could measure the exact volume of water absorbed by the hydrogels by using a balance to weigh the hydrogel before and after adding the water.

USEFUL QUESTIONS TO ASK THE STUDENTS:
1 Which brand of nappy do you think would be best at absorbing urine? Why do you think this?
2 Why do you think the hydrogel is able to absorb water?
3 What other factors might be important when choosing a nappy? What other factors are listed on the packaging?

HOMEWORK:
The students can research the environmental impact of disposable nappies and possible alternatives such as reusable nappies.

EXPERIMENT 42

Fair testing: How does temperature affect the rate of a reaction?

LEARNING OBJECTIVES:
Investigate how temperature affects the rate of a reaction.

INTRODUCTION:
The students react starch solution and potassium iodate solution in order to see the effect of temperature on the rate of the reaction.

USEFUL PRIOR WORK:
The students should understand the term rate of reaction.

BACKGROUND SCIENCE:
Chemical reactions occur when the particles of the reactants collide with enough energy to form new products. This energy is referred to as the activation energy. The rate of the reaction refers to the rate at which the reactants are used up and the products are formed. If the temperature of the reactants is increased this will have two effects. Firstly, the particles will have more kinetic energy, meaning they will be moving at a greater rate and therefore more likely to collide with each other. Secondly, the particles will be colliding with more energy, meaning they are more likely to reach the activation energy level when they do collide. Both of these factors will increase the rate of the reaction.

NATIONAL CURRICULUM LINKS:

Chemical reactions
- chemical reactions as the rearrangement of atoms
- representing chemical reactions using formulae and using equations.

MATERIALS NEEDED:
Beakers, water baths, measuring cylinders, timers, starch solution, potassium iodate solution.

SAFETY AND TECHNICAL NOTES:
- Potassium iodate is oxidising.
- Set up at least five temperatures for the students to test ranging from 20–60°C.
- Eye protection should be worn for this investigation.

METHOD:

To be done in advance by the teacher
Set up the water baths and set to the necessary temperatures. Place bottles or beakers of starch solution and potassium iodate solution into the water baths so they can come up to the correct temperature.

STUDENTS:

1. Select the first temperature you will be testing. Add 50ml of starch solution and 50ml of potassium iodate solution to separate beakers.
2. When you are ready, pour the contents of one beaker into the other beaker. Swirl the beaker a few times to make sure the contents are mixed. Start the timer.
3. When the colour change has occurred (the mixture will turn blue) stop the timer. Record how long the reaction took to occur. Record this in your results table.
4. Repeat the investigation for the rest of the temperatures. Record your results in your results table.

DATA COLLECTION IDEAS:

Temperature of reactants (°C)	Time taken for the reaction (s)

DIFFERENTIATION:

- **Decrease the challenge:** The students may need help with timing when the colour change has occurred.
- **Increase the challenge:** The students could also investigate the effect of concentration on reaction rate.

USEFUL QUESTIONS TO ASK THE STUDENTS:

1. What happened to the rate of the reaction when the temperature was increased? Why do you think this happened?
2. What do you think would happen to the rate of the reaction if we increased the concentration of the reactants? Why do you think this?
3. What do you think would happen to the rate of the reaction if we stirred the mixture? Why do you think this?

HOMEWORK:

The students can draw a graph of their results.

EXPERIMENT 43

Fair testing: How quickly will a puddle evaporate on a hot day?

LEARNING OBJECTIVES:
Investigate how temperature affects the rate of evaporation.

INTRODUCTION:
The students investigate how quickly a drop of propanone evaporates under different conditions.

USEFUL PRIOR WORK:
The students should be familiar with evaporation.

BACKGROUND SCIENCE:
Evaporation occurs when a liquid converts into vapour without having to reach the boiling point of the liquid. Evaporation is different from boiling in that evaporation only occurs at the surface of the liquid whereas boiling takes place throughout the liquid. This is because the particles on the surface of a liquid are only held in place by the particles below them. The forces holding them are therefore quite weak and they are able to escape from the liquid. Evaporation can technically occur at any temperature, although evaporation will be faster at higher temperatures. Other factors that will speed up the rate of evaporation are the surface area of the liquid, the larger the surface area the faster the rate of evaporation, and how much air is moving over the liquid, the more air the faster the rate of evaporation.

NATIONAL CURRICULUM LINKS:

Pure and impure substances
- simple techniques for separating mixtures: filtration, evaporation, distillation and chromatography.

MATERIALS NEEDED:
Microscope slides, propanone in bottles with a dropper, timers, beakers, kettle, access to a fridge, tongs, eye protection.

SAFETY AND TECHNICAL NOTES:
- Propanone is highly flammable and an irritant.
- The students should handle the hot microscope slides with tongs.
- Eye protection should be worn for this investigation.

METHOD:

To be done in advance by the teacher
Place some microscope slides in the fridge before the start of the investigation. Keep them in the fridge until they are needed. Prepare the beakers of warm water and hot water for the microscope slides to be kept in if the students will not be doing this themselves.

STUDENTS:

1. Place one drop of propanone onto a clean, dry microscope slide.
2. Time how long the propanone took to evaporate. Record this in your results table under 'room temperature'.
3. Repeat the investigation but use a microscope slide that has been kept in the fridge. Record this in your results table under 'cold'.
4. Repeat the investigation but use a microscope slide that has been kept in a beaker of water from the hot tap. Record this in your results table under 'warm'.
5. Repeat the investigation but use a microscope slide that has been kept in a beaker of boiling water. Use tongs to handle the microscope slide. Record this in your results table under 'hot'.

DATA COLLECTION IDEAS:

Temp. of slide (°C)	Time taken for propanone to evaporate (s)

DIFFERENTIATION:

- **Decrease the challenge:** The students can work in small groups with each group investigating one condition. The results can then be pooled at the end of the investigation.
- **Increase the challenge:** The students could also investigate the effect of air movement by blowing across the drop of propanone for different amounts of time.

USEFUL QUESTIONS TO ASK THE STUDENTS:

1. Which conditions produced the fastest rate of evaporation? Why do you think this was?
2. How is evaporation different from boiling?
3. What would be the best weather conditions to have when drying washing outside?

HOMEWORK:

The students can draw a graph of their results.

EXPERIMENT 44

Pattern seeking:
How quickly will a battery run down?

LEARNING OBJECTIVES:
Investigate whether the length of time a battery is charged for affects how quickly it discharges.

INTRODUCTION:
The students build a model lead-acid battery and the time it is charged for is compared with how long it takes to discharge the battery.

USEFUL PRIOR WORK:
The students should know what batteries are and how they are used.

BACKGROUND SCIENCE:
Batteries (referred to as cells when they are singular) are stores of electrochemical energy that can be used to power electric circuits. Some types of battery are rechargeable – this means that the chemical reactions taking place inside them are reversible and can continue to take place. An example of a rechargeable battery is a car battery (called a lead-acid accumulator). These types of battery are used in combustion-engine powered vehicles and electric vehicles. Although these batteries can be recharged, they often discharge ('run down') quite quickly, meaning they need to be recharged frequently. In electric vehicles this can be a problem as there can be a lack of suitable charging points for people to use. This could reduce the attractiveness of electric vehicles to consumers.

NATIONAL CURRICULUM LINKS:

Chemical reactions
- chemical reactions as the rearrangement of atoms.

MATERIALS NEEDED:
Beakers, power supply, torch bulb in holder, connecting wires, crocodile clips, timers, dilute sulphuric acid, lead foil electrodes.

SAFETY AND TECHNICAL NOTES:
- Make sure the electrodes are not touching when the model lead-acid accumulator is made.
- Sulphuric acid is an irritant.
- Lead is toxic and dangerous to the environment.
- Lead (IV) oxide is produced as a product in this investigation. Lead (IV) oxide is toxic and dangerous to the environment.
- Eye protection should be worn for this investigation.

METHOD:

To be done in advance by the teacher
Prepare a model lead-acid accumulator so the students can see the arrangement.

STUDENTS:

1 Assemble the lead-acid accumulator by following the diagram.
2 Pour dilute sulphuric acid into the beaker until it is about 3/4 full.
3 Switch on the power supply. Make sure the voltage is set to between 3 and 4 V. Allow the current to run for three minutes. This will charge up the lead-acid accumulator.
4 Disconnect the power supply and attach crocodile clips to the torch bulb. The bulb should light up as the lead-acid accumulator provides the electrical power.
5 Time how long it takes for the torch bulb to go out. Record this in your results table.
6 Repeat the investigation but charge the lead-acid accumulator up for different amounts of time.

DATA COLLECTION IDEAS:

Time taken to charge (s)	Time taken to discharge (s)

DIFFERENTIATION:
- **Decrease the challenge:** The students might need help with assembling their lead-acid accumulator.
- **Increase the challenge:** The students can also examine the electrodes at the end of the investigation to see the build up of lead (IV) oxide. They can make notes on their observations and attempt to identify the substance on the electrode.

USEFUL QUESTIONS TO ASK THE STUDENTS:
1 Was there any relationship between the amount of time the lead-acid accumulator was charged for and the time it took to discharge? Why do you think this was?
2 Do you think there are any environmental concerns with using lead-acid accumulators? Why do you think this?
3 What are the advantages and disadvantages of using electric-powered vehicles?

HOMEWORK:
The students can research other types of batteries, such as those found in mobile phones, including how they work.

EXPERIMENT 45

Pattern seeking: What is the hardest liquid to swim through?

LEARNING OBJECTIVES:
Investigate whether it is harder to swim through liquids that have a high viscosity.

INTRODUCTION:
The students compare how quickly an air bubble passes through liquids of different viscosities.

USEFUL PRIOR WORK:
The students should know what viscosity means.

BACKGROUND SCIENCE:
The viscosity of a liquid refers to the thickness of a liquid. Liquids with a high viscosity are thick and take a long time to pour. Examples of liquids with high viscosities include treacle and syrup. Liquids with a low viscosity are thinner and are easier to pour. Examples of liquids with a low viscosity include water and washing-up liquid. Objects will travel more slowly through liquids with a high viscosity compared with liquids with a low viscosity due to the extra resistance provided by the liquid. Viscosity is different from density, another property of liquids, as density refers to how many particles are present in a given volume of the liquid. A liquid can be dense but have a low viscosity and vice-versa. The viscosity of a liquid can be changed by heating the liquid; increasing the temperature will generally lower the viscosity of a liquid.

NATIONAL CURRICULUM LINKS:

The particulate nature of matter
- the properties of the different states of matter (solid, liquid and gas) in terms of the particle model, including gas pressure.

MATERIALS NEEDED:
Clear non-bendable straws, glue, different liquids to test (for example, water, milk, undiluted squash, washing-up liquid, cooking oil, shampoo, treacle etc.), timers.

SAFETY AND TECHNICAL NOTES:
- Be aware of any allergies.
- Remind the students not to consume any of the liquids.

METHOD:

To be done in advance by the teacher
Prepare the straws that will be used in the investigation. Seal one end of the straw with glue. When dried, fill the straw with one of the liquids, leaving a gap of about 1cm at the other end. Seal the other end with glue and leave to dry. Stand the straws upright in a beaker. Look up the viscosities of the liquids you will be using in the investigation for the students to use.

STUDENTS:

1 Select the first liquid you will be testing. Record its viscosity in your results table.
2 Take a straw containing that liquid. Hold it upright so that the air bubble is at the top of the straw.
3 Turn the straw upside down and start your timer. Time how long it takes for the air bubble to reach the top of the straw.
4 Repeat for the rest of the liquids.

DATA COLLECTION IDEAS:

Liquid	Time taken for bubble to travel through (s)

DIFFERENTIATION:
- **Decrease the challenge:** The students can be given help with timing the air bubble.
- **Increase the challenge:** The students can investigate whether the temperature of the liquid affects how long the air bubble takes to travel through it by comparing the results of straws of liquid that were kept in the fridge.

USEFUL QUESTIONS TO ASK THE STUDENTS:
1 Which liquid would be the easiest/hardest to swim through? How do you know this?
2 Was there any relationship between the viscosity of the liquid and the time it took the air bubble to travel through the liquid? Why do you think this was?
3 Do you think there are any ways we could change the viscosity of a liquid?

HOMEWORK:
The students can draw a graph of their results.

EXPERIMENT 46

Pattern seeking: Will aquatic plants grow in acidic water?

LEARNING OBJECTIVES:
Investigate the effect of acid rain on the growth of aquatic plants.

INTRODUCTION:
The students compare how well aquatic plants grow in increasingly acidic conditions.

USEFUL PRIOR WORK:
The students should know what acid rain is and how it is caused.

BACKGROUND SCIENCE:
Acid rain is caused when chemical pollutants in the atmosphere are absorbed by water in the atmosphere. This water will eventually fall as rain that contains these chemical pollutants. The most common pollutants are sulphur dioxide, nitrogen oxide and carbon dioxide. The pollutants lower the pH of the rainwater leading to rain that is more acidic than normal. The typical pH of acid rain is about 5.6. Acid rain can cause damage to both biological organisms and physical structures. One of the most common problems of acid rain is the fact that it can lower the pH of ponds, lakes and streams and therefore damage the wildlife that lives there. This can include small wildlife such as pond snails as well as larger wildlife such as fish. Plants that live in water can also be affected, with damage occurring to leaves that can eventually lead to the plant dying.

NATIONAL CURRICULUM LINKS:

Earth and atmosphere
- the production of carbon dioxide by human activity and the impact on climate.

MATERIALS NEEDED:
Duckweed plants, beakers, measuring cylinders, data-loggers with pH sensor or pH testing strips, white vinegar, pipettes, distilled water, labels.

SAFETY AND TECHNICAL NOTES:
- This investigation needs to be carried out over several days.
- The aim for the investigation is to make conditions that are only slightly acidic as this more accurately reflects acid rain. The students should aim for acidic levels between 5.0 and 6.75.
- Use distilled water for the investigation to reduce the number of chemicals present that may affect the results.

METHOD:

To be done in advance by the teacher
Make sure each duckweed plant has two leaves. Remove any additional leaves and discard any plants with only one leaf.

STUDENTS:

1 Set up six beakers. Label the beakers 1–6. Add 500ml of distilled water to each beaker.
2 Label beaker 1 'control'. This beaker will not have any acid added to it.
3 Use the pipette to add drops of white vinegar to each of the remaining beakers. Your aim is to make a range of acidic conditions ranging from 6.75–5.0. Use the pH sensor to measure the pH levels of the beakers. Record the pH level of each beaker on the label.
4 Add five duckweed plants to each beaker. Handle them carefully so they are not damaged.
5 Place your beakers somewhere safe, warm and light. Check your beakers each day for five days and count the number of leaves on the duckweed plants. Record the number of leaves in each beaker.

DATA COLLECTION IDEAS:

pH of water	Number of leaves present				
	Day 1	Day 2	Day 3	Day 4	Day 5

DIFFERENTIATION:
- **Decrease the challenge:** The students can be given help counting the number of leaves in the beakers.
- **Increase the challenge:** The students can investigate a wider range of acidity levels.

USEFUL QUESTIONS TO ASK THE STUDENTS:
1 What happened to the duckweed plants as the acidity levels increased? Why do you think this happened?
2 Why did we have a control beaker in our investigation?
3 What other effects might acid rain have on the environment?

HOMEWORK:
The students can produce a graph of their results.

EXPERIMENT 47

Pattern seeking: Do all oxides have the same pH?

LEARNING OBJECTIVES:
Investigate the pH of different metal and non-metal oxides.

INTRODUCTION:
The students test the pH of different metal and non-metal oxides.

USEFUL PRIOR WORK:
The students should understand the terms metal oxides and non-metal oxides.

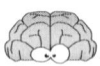

BACKGROUND SCIENCE:
This investigation allows students to test the soluble oxides of metals and the oxides of non-metals with universal indicator solution in order to determine their pH. An oxide is a compound that contains oxygen. A metal oxide is a compound that contains a metal and oxygen whilst a non-metal oxide will contain a non-metal and oxygen. In terms of pH, metal oxides are typically basic (alkaline) and non-metal oxides are acidic. These metal and non-metal oxides can also react with water. If a non-metal reacts with water it will form an acidic solution. If a metal oxide reacts with water it will form an alkaline solution. Not all metal oxides react with water however, and in those cases the resulting test with universal indicator would show as neutral.

NATIONAL CURRICULUM LINKS:

The periodic table
- the chemical properties of metal and non-metal oxides with respect to acidity.

Materials
- the order of metals and carbon in the reactivity series.

MATERIALS NEEDED:
Test tubes, test tube rack, measuring cylinder, universal indicator, pH colour chart, nitric (V) acid, phosphoric (V) acid, potassium hydroxide, sulphuric (VI) acid, sodium hydroxide, limewater, eye protection.

SAFETY AND TECHNICAL NOTES:

- Nitric (V) acid, potassium hydroxide and sodium hydroxide are irritants.
- Concentrations of 01.M or 0.2M will be suitable for this investigation.
- Universal indicator is flammable.
- Eye protection should be worn for this investigation.

METHOD:

To be done in advance by the teacher
Label the solutions that will be tested as 'oxide and water', for example, nitrogen oxide and water for nitric (V) acid.

STUDENTS:

1. Set up a test tube rack with six text tubes.
2. Add 20ml of each of the samples you will be testing to separate test tubes.
3. Add three drops of universal indicator solution to each test tube. Observe the colour of the indicator. Record the colour in your results table.
4. Use a pH colour chart to determine the pH of each sample. Record this in your results table.

DATA COLLECTION IDEAS:

Oxide	pH

DIFFERENTIATION:

- **Decrease the challenge:** The students can use a data-logger with a pH sensor to test the pH of the oxides.
- **Increase the challenge:** The students can write reaction equations showing how the different oxides are formed.

USEFUL QUESTIONS TO ASK THE STUDENTS:

1. What did you notice about the pHs of the metal oxides and the non-metal oxides?
2. Why is universal indicator more useful than simply testing whether something is an acid or an alkali?
3. What do you think would happen if we tested a metal oxide that does not react with water?

HOMEWORK:

The students can research the uses of the metal and non-metal oxides they tested in the investigation.

EXPERIMENT 48

Pattern seeking: Which element in group 2 of the periodic table is the most reactive?

LEARNING OBJECTIVES:
Investigate the pattern in reactivity of group 2 metals.

INTRODUCTION:
The students react magnesium and calcium with hydrochloric acid to see which metal is the most reactive.

USEFUL PRIOR WORK:
The students should know the basic structure of the periodic table.

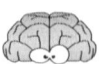

BACKGROUND SCIENCE:
The periodic table is an arrangement of all known elements according to their atomic number (the number of protons found in the nucleus). The vertical columns in the periodic table are called groups and the horizontal rows are called periods. The group 2 metals are an example of a group and are referred to as the alkaline Earth metals. The reactivity of the elements in group 2 increases as you move down the group. This increase in reactivity is due to the fact that the outermost electron of the element is further away from the nucleus (the nucleus contains protons that are positively charged), meaning that the element is able to give up this electron more easily. This effect is referred to as electron shielding.

NATIONAL CURRICULUM LINKS:

The periodic table
- the varying physical and chemical properties of different elements
- the principles underpinning the Mendeleev periodic table
- the periodic table: periods and groups; metals and non-metals
- how patterns in reactions can be predicted with reference to the periodic table.

Materials
- the order of metals and carbon in the reactivity series.

MATERIALS NEEDED:
Test tube racks, test tubes, funnels, splints, magnesium ribbon, calcium, dilute hydrochloric acid, eye protection.

SAFETY AND TECHNICAL NOTES:
- Use short lengths of magnesium ribbon. About 1cm will be sufficient.
- Use small pieces of calcium.
- Hydrochloric acid is an irritant.
- Magnesium is highly flammable.
- Calcium is flammable.
- Eye protection should be worn for this investigation.

METHOD:

To be done in advance by the teacher
Set up a Bunsen burner at the front of the room for the students to use for the hydrogen test.

STUDENTS:

1 Set up a test tube rack with two test tubes.
2 Fill each test tube about 1/4 full with hydrochloric acid. Use a funnel to prevent any spillages.
3 Add the magnesium ribbon to one test tube and the calcium to the other test tube. Observe and record what happens.
4 Add another piece of magnesium ribbon to the test tube containing the magnesium. Put your finger over the top of the test tube. When you can feel pressure building up in the test tube, place a lighted splint into the top of the test tube. Record what happens.

DATA COLLECTION IDEAS:
The students can make notes on their observations.

DIFFERENTIATION:
- **Decrease the challenge:** The students might need help with recording their observations.
- **Increase the challenge:** The students can write the equations for the reactions in the investigation.

USEFUL QUESTIONS TO ASK THE STUDENTS:
1 Which metal is more reactive – magnesium or calcium? How do you know this?
2 What does this indicate about the reactivity of the group 2 metals?
3 Which metal do you think is the most reactive and least reactive in group 2? Why do you think this?

HOMEWORK:
The students can research the work of Mendeleev on the periodic table.

EXPERIMENT 49

Pattern seeking: Which element in group 7 of the periodic table is the most reactive?

LEARNING OBJECTIVES:
Investigate the pattern in reactivity of halogens as you move down group 7.

INTRODUCTION:
The students use universal indicator paper to test halogen solutions before performing some displacement reactions.

USEFUL PRIOR WORK:
The students should know the basic structure of the periodic table.

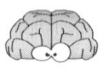

BACKGROUND SCIENCE:
The name halogens is given to the group 7 elements in the periodic table (a group is the name given to a vertical column in the periodic table). The halogens are highly reactive, non-metals that form acidic compounds when they are reacted with hydrogen that can be used to make salt (halogen means 'salt former'). They also react very vigorously with the group 1 elements (this is due to the fact that group 1 elements have one electron in their outer shell, whilst the halogens have seven, therefore the group 1 elements can easily give off their one electron to the halogens, giving the halogen a full outer shell of eight electrons). The halogens become less reactive as you move down the group.

NATIONAL CURRICULUM LINKS:

The periodic table
- the varying physical and chemical properties of different elements
- the principles underpinning the Mendeleev periodic table
- the periodic table: periods and groups; metals and non-metals
- how patterns in reactions can be predicted with reference to the periodic table
- the properties of metals and non-metals.

MATERIALS NEEDED:
Test tubes, test tube racks, spotting tiles, pipettes, universal indicator, potassium bromide solution, potassium iodide solution, potassium chloride, chlorine solution, bromine solution, iodine solution.

SAFETY AND TECHNICAL NOTES:
- Perform this investigation in a well ventilated room.
- Chlorine solution is an irritant.
- Bromine solution is harmful and an irritant.
- Do not allow students to inhale the chlorine gas.
- Eye protection should be worn for this investigation.

METHOD:

To be done in advance by the teacher
Open any windows to ensure the room is well ventilated.

STUDENTS:

1. Place three pieces of universal indicator paper into separate dimples on a spotting tile.
2. Use a pipette to place a few drops of chlorine solution onto one of the pieces of indicator paper. Observe and record what happens.
3. Use a pipette to place a few drops of bromine solution onto one of the pieces of indicator paper. Observe and record what happens.
4. Use a pipette to place a few drops of iodine solution onto one of the pieces of indicator paper. Observe and record what happens.
5. Set up a test tube rack with six test tubes.
6. In the first test tube, add a small amount of chlorine solution and a small amount of potassium bromide. Observe and record what happens.
7. In the second test tube, add a small amount of chlorine solution and a small amount of potassium iodide. Observe and record what happens.
8. In the third test tube, add a small amount of bromine solution and a small amount of potassium chloride. Observe and record what happens.
9. In the fourth test tube, add a small amount of bromine solution and a small amount of potassium iodide. Observe and record what happens.
10. In the fifth test tube, add a small amount of iodine solution and a small amount of potassium chloride. Observe and record what happens.
11. In the sixth test tube, add a small amount of iodine solution and a small amount of potassium bromide. Observe and record what happens.

DATA COLLECTION IDEAS:
The students can make notes on their observations.

DIFFERENTIATION:
- **Decrease the challenge:** The students can just perform the tests with universal indicator paper.
- **Increase the challenge:** The students can attempt to write equations for the reactions in the investigation.

USEFUL QUESTIONS TO ASK THE STUDENTS:
1. What happened to the reactivity of the halogens as you moved down the group? How do you know this?
2. What happened when you reacted the different halogens together? Why do you think this happened?
3. Can you think of any everyday uses for the halogens?

HOMEWORK:
The students can research the uses of the halogens that they used in the investigation.

EXPERIMENT 50

Classification and identification: Are all changes reversible?

LEARNING OBJECTIVES:
Classify some everyday changes as either reversible or irreversible.

INTRODUCTION:
The students carry out a set of mini investigations and classify the resulting changes as either reversible or irreversible.

USEFUL PRIOR WORK:
The students should know what reversible and irreversible reactions are.

BACKGROUND SCIENCE:
Reactions can be either physical or chemical. Physical reactions involve a substance or substances changing their physical state, for example a solid melting and changing state to a liquid. Physical reactions are typically reversible as the physical changes can be undone. A chemical reaction involves substances reacting together in order to form new products. Chemical reactions can be reversible or irreversible. If the reactants are not used up in the reaction then the reaction is reversible. An example is ammonium chloride breaking down into ammonia and hydrogen chloride. If the reactants are used up in the reaction then the reaction is irreversible. An example is burning petrol.

NATIONAL CURRICULUM LINKS:

The particulate nature of matter
- the properties of the different states of matter (solid, liquid and gas) in terms of the particle model, including gas pressure
- changes of state in terms of the particle model.

Chemical reactions
- chemical reactions as the rearrangement of atoms.

MATERIALS NEEDED:
Bunsen burners, candles, sand trays, splints, foil trays, tongs, toaster, kettle, beakers, bread, chocolate, eggs, iron filings, graph paper, Vaseline, balance.

SAFETY AND TECHNICAL NOTES:
- This investigation can be set up as a circuit of mini investigations that the students work through.
- The students should wear eye protection for this investigation.
- For the candle investigation, the candle should be placed in a sand tray and lit using a splint. Set up a Bunsen burner for the students to light the splint.

METHOD:

To be done in advance by the teacher
Have a Bunsen burner set up in a safe location for the students to use to light their splints.

Are all changes reversible? 103

STUDENTS:

For each investigation, write down your observations before, during and after the reaction. Identify any reactions taking place in the investigations and decide if they are reversible or irreversible.

Burning candle
1. Place the candle in the sand tray. Light the candle using the splint. Observe the candle.
2. Blow out the candle. Observe the candle.

Making toast
1. Draw around a slice of bread onto some graph paper. Weigh the slice of bread using the balance.
2. Put the bread in the toaster for one minute.
3. Draw around the slice of bread again onto the same piece of graph paper. Weigh the slice of bread using the balance.

Melting chocolate
1. Set up a Bunsen burner.
2. Put a small piece of chocolate into the foil tray and use the tongs to hold the foil tray just above the flame.
3. Hold the foil tray over the flame until the chocolate has melted.
4. When the chocolate has melted, move the foil tray away from the Bunsen burner.

Boiling eggs
1. Boil the kettle.
2. Add 300ml of the boiling water to a beaker.
3. Carefully crack the egg over the beaker so the egg falls into the boiling water.

Homemade sparklers
1. Set up a Bunsen burner.
2. Coat the end of a splint with Vaseline.
3. Dip the Vaseline into the iron filings.
4. Put the Bunsen burner onto the blue flame and hold the splint in the top of the flame.

DATA COLLECTION IDEAS:

Change	Observations	Reversible or irreversible?

DIFFERENTIATION:
- **Decrease the challenge:** The students can work in groups with each group carrying out one investigation. The results can be pooled at the end of the investigation.
- **Increase the challenge:** The students can carry out a more complex reversible reaction, for example recovering salt that has been dissolved in water.

USEFUL QUESTIONS TO ASK THE STUDENTS:
1. Which reactions were reversible/irreversible? How did you know this?
2. Did any investigations contain both reversible and irreversible changes?
3. What other examples of reversible and irreversible reactions can you think of?

HOMEWORK:
The students can find examples of other everyday reversible and irreversible reactions.

EXPERIMENT 51

Classification and identification: What is the best soil for growing plants?

LEARNING OBJECTIVES:
Classify different soil samples and select the best soil for growing different plants.

INTRODUCTION:
The students compare different soil samples based on particular characteristics and use this information to decide which plants should be grown in each soil.

USEFUL PRIOR WORK:
The students should know what factors plants need in order to grow.

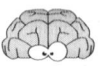

BACKGROUND SCIENCE:
Soil is formed from rocks broken down via weathering and decayed organic matter. Soil can vary in its composition due to the types of, and ratios of, rocks and organic matter it has formed from. Generally, soil is classed as sandy, clay or loam. Sandy soils have high levels of sandy particles and tend to be very dry with water draining through them quickly. Clay soils have high levels of clay particles and tend to be dense with water not draining through them. Loam soils have a mix of both sand and clay particles, forming a soil that can hold some water but also allow it to drain through the soil. Loam soil is generally considered to be the best type of soil for growing plants. Soil can also vary in its pH due to the concentration of minerals in the soil and also due to external factors such as the presence of acid rain. Some plants prefer growing in acidic soils, for example foxgloves and heathers, whereas others prefer an alkaline soil, for example, cabbages and cauliflowers.

NATIONAL CURRICULUM LINKS:

Earth and atmosphere
- the composition of the Earth
- the structure of the Earth
- the rock cycle and the formation of igneous, sedimentary and metamorphic rocks.

MATERIALS NEEDED:
Sand and pottery clay for comparisons, samples of different types of soil (one sandy/gritty soil, one clay soil, one loam soil with high acidity, one loam soil with high alkalinity, one neutral loam soil), magnifying lenses, measuring cylinders, beakers, white tiles, funnels, measuring spoons, filter paper, soil pH testing kit or data-loggers with pH meters, water, timers.

SAFETY AND TECHNICAL NOTES:
- The students should wash their hands after the investigation.
- The following plants can be used as examples in this investigation: California poppy – sandy soil; hydrangea – clay soil; rhododendrons – acidic soil; alpine pinks – alkaline soil; broccoli – neutral soil.

METHOD:

To be done in advance by the teacher
Prepare the soil samples that will be used.

STUDENTS:

1. Examine each soil sample using the magnifying lens. Compare the colour and particles of the soil samples. Use the sand and clay examples you have been given to help your observations. Record your observations.
2. Rub a small amount of each soil sample between your fingers. Compare the different textures. Use the sand and clay examples you have been given to help your observations. Record your observations.
3. Place a small amount of each soil into a different well in a spotting tile. Use the soil pH testing kit or data-logger to find the pH of each soil sample. Record your observations.
4. Fold a piece of filter paper and place it in a funnel. Place the funnel into a beaker.
5. Add a tablespoon of one soil sample to the funnel. Measure out 100ml of water. Pour the water into the funnel and start the timer. Time for one minute then measure how much water has passed through the soil. Record this measurement.
6. Using your results, decide which soil sample would be best for growing the different plant species.

DATA COLLECTION IDEAS:

Soil sample	Observations

DIFFERENTIATION:
- **Decrease the challenge:** The students can work in groups with each group looking at one soil sample. The results can then be pooled at the end of the investigation.
- **Increase the challenge:** The students can research different plant species themselves in order to decide which plants would grow in the different soils.

USEFUL QUESTIONS TO ASK THE STUDENTS:
1. What similarities and differences were there between the different soil samples?
2. Why do you think different plants species prefer to grow in different types of soil?
3. What other factors might affect the quality of the soil?

HOMEWORK:
The students can research how soil is formed and produce an annotated flow diagram.

EXPERIMENT 52

Classification and identification: How can we identify colourless gases?

LEARNING OBJECTIVES:
Learn how to identify three different gases.

INTRODUCTION:
The students learn how to identify the gases carbon dioxide, oxygen and hydrogen.

USEFUL PRIOR WORK:
The students should know what a gas is and the names of some common gases.

BACKGROUND SCIENCE:
This investigation allows students to produce small amounts of a particular gas and carry out the standard test for identifying that gas. The gases being investigated are hydrogen, oxygen and carbon dioxide. First, the students will produce small quantities of the gases. In order to produce hydrogen the students will add a small strip of magnesium to a test tube containing hydrochloric acid. In order to produce oxygen the students will add manganese dioxide to a solution of hydrogen peroxide. In order to produce carbon dioxide the students will add marble chips to hydrochloric acid. In terms of testing for the gases, hydrogen will cause a popping sound if a lighted wooden splint is placed in a test tube containing hydrogen, oxygen will cause a glowing wooden splint to relight in a test tube containing oxygen and carbon dioxide will turn limewater milky when it is bubbled through.

NATIONAL CURRICULUM LINKS:

Pure and impure substances
- the identification of pure substances.

MATERIALS NEEDED:
Strips of magnesium (approximately 2cm long), hydrochloric acid, marble chips, limewater, manganese dioxide, hydrogen peroxide, measuring cylinder, conical flask with bung and delivery tube, test tubes, test tube racks, Bunsen burners, heat-proof mats, pipettes, water troughs, spatulas, wooden splints, eye protection.

SAFETY AND TECHNICAL NOTES:
- Hydrochloric acid is an irritant.
- Hydrogen peroxide is low hazard.
- Manganese dioxide is harmful so should be kept with the teacher and only required amounts distributed to the students.
- Eye protection should be worn for this investigation.

METHOD:

To be done in advance by the teacher

You may want to prepare a hydrogen balloon to ignite as a demonstration for the students to compare with their test for hydrogen. This can be linked to the Hindenburg disaster (see homework section).

STUDENTS:

Identifying hydrogen

1. Place a test tube in a test tube rack. Add 10cm^3 of hydrochloric acid to the test tube.
2. Set up a Bunsen burner and place it on the safety flame.
3. Light a wooden splint using the Bunsen burner and add a strip of magnesium to the hydrochloric acid in the test tube.
4. Place the lit wooden splint into the top half of the test tube (do not let it touch the hydrochloric acid). Record what happens.

Identifying oxygen

1. Place a test tube in a test tube rack. Add 10cm^3 of hydrogen peroxide to the test tube.
2. Set up a Bunsen burner and place it on the safety flame.
3. Light a wooden splint using the Bunsen burner then blow it out so that the end of the splint is glowing red but there is no flame present.
4. Add a spatula full of manganese dioxide to the test tube. When it starts bubbling place the glowing splint into the top half of the test tube (do not let it touch the hydrogen peroxide). Record what happens.

Identifying carbon dioxide

1. Half fill a boiling tube with limewater. Place the boiling tube into a test tube rack. Place the bung with the delivery tube into the top of the boiling tube.
2. Add 20cm^3 of hydrochloric acid to a conical flask. Add a spatula full of marble chips to the conical flask.
3. Place the other bung on the delivery tube into the conical flask. Record what happens.

DATA COLLECTION IDEAS:

The students can record the positive results they obtained for each identification test and produce instructions on how to carry out the tests.

DIFFERENTIATION:

- **Decrease the challenge:** The materials can be measured out for the students for each test.
- **Increase the challenge:** The students could also try collecting the carbon dioxide they produce using an upturned test tube in a water trough.

USEFUL QUESTIONS TO ASK THE STUDENTS:

1. What was the positive result for each identification test? What else did you observe happening in the tests?
2. What types of reaction were present in each identification test?
3. Can you think of any other ways we could make hydrogen?

HOMEWORK:

The students can research the Hindenburg disaster and the role that hydrogen gas played.

EXPERIMENT 53

Classification and identification: How can polymers be identified?

LEARNING OBJECTIVES:
Determine how we can identify different polymers.

INTRODUCTION:
The students use known densities of liquids to identify unknown samples of polymers by observing whether they float or sink in the liquid.

USEFUL PRIOR WORK:
The students should know what a polymer is and some examples.

BACKGROUND SCIENCE:
A polymer is a substance that is made up of repeating units of monomers (two or more carbon atoms that are chemically bonded). Plastic is an example of a polymer. There are several different types of plastic, all of which exhibit different properties. The six most common everyday plastics are: polyethylene terephthalate (PET), used to make plastic bottles such as those used for fizzy drinks; high-density polyethylene (HDPE), used to make thicker plastic bottles such as milk bottles as well as plastic carrier bags; polyvinyl chloride (PVC), used to make bottles for household cleaners such as bleach; low-density polyethylene (LDPE), used to make flexile items such as plastic sandwich bags and squeezy bottles; polypropylene (PP), used to make yogurt pots and microwavable containers, and polystyrene (PS), used to make plastic cups and take-away containers. The different plastics can be identified by observing whether they float or sink in liquids with known densities.

NATIONAL CURRICULUM LINKS:

Materials
- properties of ceramics, polymers and composites (qualitative).

MATERIALS NEEDED:
Beakers, tongs, stirring rods, measuring cylinders, isopropyl rubbing alcohol (70% vol), golden syrup, samples of the six plastic polymers (see background science).

SAFETY AND TECHNICAL NOTES:
- The density ranges for the plastics are as follows: PET: 1.38–1.40, HDPE: 0.94–0.96, PVC: 1.20–1.55, LDPE: 0.91–0.93, PP: 0.89–0.91, PS: 1.04–1.11.
- The densities of the liquids used in the investigation are as follows: water: 1.0 g/ml, golden syrup: 1.40 g/ml, liquid 1: 0.91 g/ml, liquid 2: 0.93g/ml, liquid 3: 1.16 g/ml.
- Isopropyl rubbing alcohol is flammable.
- Remind the students not to consume the golden syrup.
- The students should wear eye protection for this investigation.
- Ensure that any containers that stored food or cleaning products have been empty and cleaned.
- The students should wash their hands after the investigation.

METHOD:

To be done in advance by the teacher

Prepare samples of the plastics the students will be using in the investigation – about 1cm² of each plastic will be sufficient.

STUDENTS:

1. Examine the plastics you will be testing. Record your observations in your results table.
2. Prepare the liquids you will be using for your investigation as follows:
3. Liquid 1: Add 50ml of water to a beaker. Density = 1.0 g/ml
4. Liquid 2: Add 50ml of alcohol and 20ml of water to a beaker. Density = 0.91 g/ml
5. Liquid 3: Add 40ml of alcohol and 20ml of water to a beaker. Density = 0.93 g/ml
6. Liquid 4: Add 20ml of golden syrup and 20ml of water to a beaker. Density = 1.16 g/ml
7. Liquid 5: Add 40ml of golden syrup to a beaker. Density = 1.40 g/ml
8. Add all of your plastic samples to liquid 1. Observe whether they float or sink and record the results in your table.
9. Remove the samples from the beaker using the tongs. Rinse them under the tap and dry them off using paper towels.
10. Repeat steps 3 and 4 for the rest of the liquids.
11. Using your results from the investigation, see if you can identify which type of plastic each sample comes from.

DATA COLLECTION IDEAS:

Sample	Floats or sinks in liquid 1?	Floats or sinks in liquid 2?	Floats or sinks in liquid 3?	Floats or sinks in liquid 4?	Floats or sinks in liquid 5?	Type of plastic

DIFFERENTIATION:

- **Decrease the challenge:** The liquids used in the investigation can be prepared for the students.
- **Increase the challenge:** The students could perform additional tests to aid identification of the plastics such as flame tests.

USEFUL QUESTIONS TO ASK THE STUDENTS:

1. Were you able to identify all the plastics? How were you able to do this?
2. Why is it important to be able to identify different types of plastic?
3. Is there any way we could improve or extend this investigation?

HOMEWORK:

The students could research the impact of plastics on the environment.

EXPERIMENT 54

Classification and identification: Do chemical reactions always give off heat?

LEARNING OBJECTIVES:
Classify a selection of chemical reactions as either exothermic or endothermic.

INTRODUCTION:
The students measure the temperature changes in four different reactions in order to classify them as either endothermic or exothermic reactions.

USEFUL PRIOR WORK:
The students should understand what energy is and that energy cannot be created or destroyed but only transferred from one type of energy to another.

BACKGROUND SCIENCE:
Chemical reactions can be either exothermic or endothermic. Exothermic reactions transfer energy, usually in the form of heat, to their surroundings. Endothermic reactions take in energy, usually in the form of heat, from their surroundings. Whether a chemical reaction is exothermic or endothermic depends on the bonds that are being broken and formed during the reaction. Breaking bonds is an endothermic process, whereas forming bonds is an exothermic reaction. If more energy is given off from forming new bonds than was used by breaking down bonds then the reaction will be exothermic. The temperature change during the reaction can be measured in order to determine if the reaction is exothermic or endothermic. Examples of exothermic reactions are burning and neutralisation. Examples of endothermic reactions are electrolysis and the reaction of sodium carbonate with an acid.

NATIONAL CURRICULUM LINKS:

Energetics
- energy changes on changes of state (qualitative)
- exothermic and endothermic chemical reactions (qualitative).

MATERIALS NEEDED:
Beakers, polystyrene cups, stirring rods, thermometers, spatulas, measuring cylinders, hydrochloric acid, sulphuric acid, sodium hydroxide, sodium hydrogencarbonate, copper (II) sulphate, magnesium powder, magnesium ribbon, citric acid, eye protection.

SAFETY AND TECHNICAL NOTES:
- All the chemicals for the investigation should be approximately 0.4M concentration.
- Magnesium powder is flammable.
- Sodium hydroxide and citric acid are irritants.
- The students should wear eye protection for this investigation.
- The students should wash their hands after the investigation.

METHOD:

To be done in advance by the teacher

Cut the magnesium ribbon into individual short lengths; approximately 3cm will be sufficient.

STUDENTS:

You will be performing four separate investigations. For each investigation record the change in temperature for the reactants and decide if the reaction is exothermic (the reaction gives off heat to its surroundings) or endothermic (the reaction takes in heat from its surroundings).

Sodium hydroxide solution and hydrochloric acid

1. Put a polystyrene cup into a beaker. The beaker will help to stabilise the polystyrene cup during the reaction.
2. Add 10cm^2 of sodium hydroxide solution to the polystyrene cup.
3. Measure the temperature of the sodium hydroxide solution in the polystyrene cup. Record this in your results table.
4. Add 10cm^2 of hydrochloric acid to the polystyrene cup. Stir with a stirring rod and then take the temperature of the mixture. Record this in your results table.

Sodium hydrogencarbonate and citric acid

1. Put a polystyrene cup into a beaker. The beaker will help to stabilise the polystyrene cup during the reaction.
2. Add 10cm^2 of sodium hydrogencarbonate to the polystyrene cup.
3. Measure the temperature of the sodium hydrogencarbonate in the polystyrene cup. Record this in your results table.
4. Add four level spatula measures of citric acid to the polystyrene cup. Stir with a stirring rod and then take the temperature of the mixture. Record this in your results table.

Sulphuric acid and magnesium ribbon

1. Put a polystyrene cup into a beaker. The beaker will help to stabilise the polystyrene cup during the reaction.
2. Add 10cm^2 of sulphuric acid to the polystyrene cup.
3. Measure the temperature of the sulphuric acid in the polystyrene cup. Record this in your results table.
4. Add one strip of magnesium ribbon to the polystyrene cup. Stir with a stirring rod and then take the temperature of the mixture. Record this in your results table.

Copper (II) sulphate solution and magnesium powder

1. Put a polystyrene cup into a beaker. The beaker will help to stabilise the polystyrene cup during the reaction.
2. Add 10cm^2 of copper (II) sulphate solution to the polystyrene cup.
3. Measure the temperature of the copper (II) sulphate in the polystyrene cup. Record this in your results table.
4. Add one level spatula measure of magnesium powder to the polystyrene cup. Stir with a stirring rod and then take the temperature of the mixture. Record this in your results table.

DATA COLLECTION IDEAS:

Reaction	Temp. of reactants (°C)	Temp. during reaction (°C)	Exothermic or endothermic?

DIFFERENTIATION:
- **Decrease the challenge:** The students can work in small groups with each group investigating one reaction. The results can then be pooled at the end of the investigation.
- **Increase the challenge:** The students can record the temperature of the reactions every 10 seconds in order to see the rate of temperature change.

USEFUL QUESTIONS TO ASK THE STUDENTS:
1. Which reactions were exothermic/endothermic? How did you know this?
2. Why do you think some reactions need to take energy in from their surroundings?
3. Can you think of any other examples of exothermic or endothermic reactions?

HOMEWORK:
The students can find other examples of exothermic and endothermic reactions.

EXPERIMENT 55

Classification and identification: Does everything dissolve in water?

LEARNING OBJECTIVES:
Identify the correct solvent for a variety of different solutes.

INTRODUCTION:
The students investigate which solutes will dissolve in a selection of different solvents.

USEFUL PRIOR WORK:
The students should understand the terms solute and solvent.

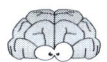

BACKGROUND SCIENCE:
Solute is the name given to a substance that will dissolve in a solvent (a liquid). Different solutes will dissolve in different solvents. This is due to the polarity (polar or non-polar) exhibited by both the solute and the solvent. Solvents that are polar will only dissolve polar solutes, whilst solvents that are non-polar will only dissolve non-polar solutes. The phrase 'like dissolves like' is used to describe this principle. An example of a polar solvent is water. Examples of non-polar solvents are vegetable oil and acetone. Sugar is an example of a polar solute that dissolves in water but not vegetable oil or acetone. Lipstick is a non-polar solute that dissolves in acetone. Wax is another non-polar solute and will dissolve in vegetable oil. Some substances will not dissolve in any naturally occurring solvent, an example is sand.

NATIONAL CURRICULUM LINKS:

Pure and impure substances
- mixtures, including dissolving.

MATERIALS NEEDED:
Beakers, measuring cylinders, measuring spoons, cotton wool buds, sugar, salt, sand, wax, vegetable oil, nail polish remover, nail polish, water.

SAFETY AND TECHNICAL NOTES:
- Use nail polish remover that contains acetone. This will be listed on the ingredients.
- Acetone is flammable.
- For the nail polish test, dip one end of a cotton wool bud in nail polish and leave it to dry overnight. It is best to use a bright colour to make the observations easier.
- For the wax test, grate small pieces of wax from a candle.

METHOD:

To be done in advance by the teacher
Prepare the nail polish and the wax tests (see safety and technical notes).

STUDENTS:

1 Add 250ml of warm water from the hot tap to a beaker. Label this beaker 'water'.
2 Add 250ml of vegetable oil to a beaker. Label this beaker 'vegetable oil'.
3 Add 250ml of acetone to a beaker. Label this beaker 'acetone'.
4 Add 1 teaspoon of sugar to each beaker and stir. Record whether the sugar dissolves in your results table.
5 Add 1 teaspoon of salt to each beaker and stir. Record whether the salt dissolves in your results table.
6 Add 1 teaspoon of wax to each beaker and stir. Record whether the wax dissolves in your results table.
7 Add 1 teaspoon of sand to each beaker and stir. Record whether the sand dissolves in your results table.
8 Dip a cotton wool bud painted with nail varnish into each beaker. Record whether the nail varnish dissolves in your results table.

DATA COLLECTION IDEAS:

DIFFERENTIATION:

Substance	Does it dissolve in water?	Does it dissolve in vegetable oil?	Does it dissolve in acetone?

- **Decrease the challenge:** The students can work in small groups with each group investigating one solvent. The results can then be pooled at the end of the investigation.
- **Increase the challenge:** The students could choose some of their own solutes to test. Make sure any choices are safe.

USEFUL QUESTIONS TO ASK THE STUDENTS:

1 Which solutes dissolved in which solvent? Were you surprised by any of your results?
2 Why do you think some solutes did not dissolve in some solvents?
3 What other solutes do you think would dissolve in water/vegetable oil/acetone? Why do you think this?

HOMEWORK:

The students can research dry cleaning and how stains from fabric can be removed without the need for water.

EXPERIMENT 56

Modelling: Can we make our own fizzing bath bombs?

LEARNING OBJECTIVES:
Make a fizzing bath bomb using bicarbonate of soda and citric acid.

INTRODUCTION:
The students design and make their own fizzing bath bombs based on an acid and alkali reaction.

USEFUL PRIOR WORK:
The students should know what acids and alkalis are and how they can react with each other.

BACKGROUND SCIENCE:
Bath bombs are toiletries that usually fizz when added to water and also release colour, fragrance and/or oil into the water. They work due to the reaction between acids and alkalis. In this investigation the acid is citric acid and the alkali is bicarbonate of soda. When these are added to water a reaction occurs between the acid and alkali, releasing carbon dioxide. This carbon dioxide is what causes the bath bomb to fizz and move around the water. The more carbon dioxide that the bath bomb produces, the faster it will move around the bath. The reaction has finished when the bath bomb stops fizzing. Cornstarch is sometimes added to bath bombs in order to slow down the reaction and keep the bath bomb fizzing for longer. The cornstarch is not used up in the reaction itself but simply acts as a 'filler' in the bath bomb (thus reducing the cost of producing the bath bomb).

NATIONAL CURRICULUM LINKS:

Chemical reactions
- chemical reactions as the rearrangement of atoms
- representing chemical reactions using formulae and using equations
- reactions of acids with alkalis to produce a salt plus water.

MATERIALS NEEDED:
Ice cube trays, bowls, bicarbonate of soda, citric acid, food colouring, measuring spoons, droppers, spoons, labels, plastic sandwich bags, olive or almond oil (optional), essential oils (optional).

SAFETY AND TECHNICAL NOTES:
- Any container can be used to mould the bath bombs. Moulds for making chocolates and soaps often come in interesting shapes.
- Use pre-blended essential oils that can be applied directly to the skin.
- Check for any allergies if using essential oils.
- The bath bombs need to dry overnight in a dry, non-humid environment.

METHOD:

To be done in advance by the teacher
Have somewhere to place the bath bombs to dry overnight.

STUDENTS:

1 Add 10 tablespoons of bicarbonate of soda and three tablespoons of citric acid to a bowl. Mix well and be sure to break down any lumps.
2 Choose what colour you would like to use for your bath bomb. Add 10 drops of the food colouring to the bowl and mix well.
3 Choose what fragrance you would like to use for your bath bomb. Add 10 drops of the essential oil to the bowl and mix well.
4 If you are using olive or almond oil in your bath bomb then add 10 drops to the bowl and mix well.
5 Spoon the mixture into the ice-cube tray. Level off the bath bombs using the back of the spoon. Label which bath bombs are yours and place your bath bombs somewhere safe and dry.
6 When your bath bombs have dried overnight, place them in a plastic sandwich bag to keep them dry until you use them. When you use the bath bomb, observe what happens and record how long the bath bomb fizzes for.

DATA COLLECTION IDEAS:
The students can take photographs of their bath bombs and of the steps involved in making the bath bombs.

DIFFERENTIATION:
- **Decrease the challenge:** The materials needed to make the bath bombs can be measured out for the students.
- **Increase the challenge:** The students can add cornstarch, which acts as a filler, to their bath bombs to see what effect this has on how long they fizz for. The more cornstarch that is added to the bath bomb, the longer the bath bomb will fizz for.

USEFUL QUESTIONS TO ASK THE STUDENTS:
1 What do you think will happen when the bath bomb is added to water? Why do you think this will happen?
2 What other factors do you think could affect how fast or long the bath bomb fizzes in the bath?
3 What other everyday activities involve acids and alkalis reacting?

HOMEWORK:
The students could observe their bath bombs when they are added to water and record their observations including how long the bath bomb fizzed.

EXPERIMENT 57

Modelling: Can we make popping fruit juice balls?

LEARNING OBJECTIVES:
Make our own 'popping' fruit juice balls.

INTRODUCTION:
The students use the molecular gastronomy process of spherification to make popping fruit juice balls.

USEFUL PRIOR WORK:
The students should know the particle model for states of matter.

BACKGROUND SCIENCE:
Molecular gastronomy is the science of how the molecules in food are changed as they are cooked or prepared. One particular molecular gastronomy technique is spherification. This involves turning a liquid food into small, semi-solid balls. To do this a chemical reaction between sodium alginate and calcium chloride is utilised. When these two chemicals react together they form calcium alginate, which is a gelatinous substance. This causes the food to form into small balls which 'pop' when eaten, releasing the liquid inside. Spherification is a complex chemical reaction and will only occur if the food being used is the correct pH. Foods that are too acidic, such as fruit juice, will not undergo spherification. To overcome this problem a base (alkaline solution), such as sodium citrate, can be added in order to raise the pH of the food being used in the investigation.

NATIONAL CURRICULUM LINKS:

The particulate nature of matter
- the properties of the different states of matter (solid, liquid and gas) in terms of the particle model, including gas pressure.

Chemical reactions
- chemical reactions as the rearrangement of atoms.

MATERIALS NEEDED:
Sodium alginate, calcium chloride, sodium citrate, measuring cylinders, bowls, balance, blender, timers, spoons, 50ml syringes, sieves, Milton steriliser, fruit juices for making the balls.

SAFETY AND TECHNICAL NOTES:
- Readymade kits can be purchased for carrying out this investigation.
- As this investigation will be producing food that will be consumed it is important that all surfaces and equipment are sterilised beforehand. Use a steriliser such as Milton.

METHOD:

To be done in advance by the teacher

Sterilise all surfaces and equipment that will be used in this investigation. Follow the instructions on the packaging.

STUDENTS:

1. Add 250ml of water into a beaker. Add 2g of calcium chloride to the beaker of water and stir until the calcium chloride has dissolved. Pour this mixture into a bowl.
2. Measure out 250ml of the first juice you will be using to make your popping balls. Add this to a blender. Add 2g of sodium alginate to the blender.
3. Blend the fruit juice and sodium alginate together until you have a smooth mixture.
4. Carefully pour the mixture from the blender into a beaker.
5. Use a syringe to suck up a small amount of the fruit juice mixture from the beaker. Carefully squeeze a small amount of the mixture into the bowl containing the calcium chloride solution. You only want a small drop to come out. Start the timer. The fruit juice mixture should form into a small ball.
6. After one minute has passed use the spoon to scoop out the ball. Place it on some paper towels to dry. If a ball did not form or was very soft then add 1g of sodium citrate to the fruit juice mixture. Stir with a spoon.
7. Repeat step 5 and step 6 until the fruit juice mixture forms solid balls that you are easily able to remove from the bowl.
8. Carefully put the balls into a sieve and gently rinse them under cold water to wash off the calcium chloride. Your popping fruit balls are ready to eat! If you have time you can make more popping fruit balls using a different fruit juice.

DATA COLLECTION IDEAS:

The students can take photographs of their popping fruit balls and write instructions for how to make them.

DIFFERENTIATION:

- **Decrease the challenge:** The solutions can be prepared for the students so they only need to form the balls.
- **Increase the challenge:** The students can compare different fruit juices and how much sodium citrate needs to be added for the popping balls to form.

USEFUL QUESTIONS TO ASK THE STUDENTS:

1. Which state of matter would you classify the popping balls? Why do you think this?
2. What happened when more sodium citrate was added to the mixture? Why do you think this happened?
3. Can you think of other examples of scientific processes used in cooking?

HOMEWORK:

The students could research other forms of molecular gastronomy.

EXPERIMENT 58

Modelling:
Can we grow a crystal garden?

LEARNING OBJECTIVES:
Grow our own crystals to create a crystal garden.

INTRODUCTION:
The students use metal nitrates and sulphates in order to grow silicate crystals.

USEFUL PRIOR WORK:
The students should know the rock cycle and the basic structure of the Earth.

BACKGROUND SCIENCE:
A crystal garden is formed by adding metal salts to an aqueous solution of sodium silicate (known as waterglass). Over a period of time, coloured crystals form into plant like structures within the waterglass. The longer the crystals are left for, the more they will grow. The crystals form because the transition metal salts start to dissolve in the water but then form insoluble metal silicates. These insoluble metal silicates form a solid, which is then deposited in the waterglass. The crystals typically grow upwards from the bottom of the container. The different colours of the crystals are caused by the different metals found in the metal salts. The resulting crystal garden should not be moved or shaken too much as the crystals are very delicate and will break apart quite easily.

NATIONAL CURRICULUM LINKS:

Earth and atmosphere
- the composition of the Earth
- the structure of the Earth
- the rock cycle and the formation of igneous, sedimentary and metamorphic rocks.

MATERIALS NEEDED:
Hot deionised water, sodium silicate solution, metal sulphates or nitrates such as cobalt (II) nitrate, magnesium nitrate, iron (III) nitrate and nickel nitrate, beakers, stirring rods, forceps, paper towels, eye protection, non-latex gloves.

SAFETY AND TECHNICAL NOTES:
- The students should wear eye protection and gloves for this investigation.
- Some metal nitrates and sulphates are irritant or harmful.
- Only a very small number of crystals are required to 'seed' the crystal garden.
- Crystals will begin to grow overnight but better results will be obtained by allowing the gardens to grow over a few days.

METHOD:

To be done in advance by the teacher
Have a suitable space prepared for the beakers to be stored.

STUDENTS:

1. Fill a beaker to a depth of approximately 3cm with sodium silicate solution.
2. Add deionised water to the beaker containing the sodium silicate solution. Fill the beaker to a depth of approximately 12cm.
3. Stir the beaker using a glass rod until you can no longer see two separate layers of liquid. Allow the liquid in the beaker to settle.
4. Select the first crystal you want to add to your garden. Use your forceps to pick up a few crystals and drop them into the beaker. Add the rest of the crystals you want to include in the same way. Try to ensure that the crystals do not touch each other in the beaker.
5. Cover the beakers with a paper towel and place the beaker somewhere safe. In a few days you can examine your crystal garden and see what has grown.

DATA COLLECTION IDEAS:
The students can take photographs of their completed crystal gardens.

DIFFERENTIATION:
- **Decrease the challenge:** The students can be given assistance with preparing the crystal garden.
- **Increase the challenge:** The students can add extra features to their crystal garden such as small pebbles and pipe cleaners and attempt to have the crystals grow along or around these features.

USEFUL QUESTIONS TO ASK THE STUDENTS:
1. What had happened to the crystals in your crystal garden when we observed them again? Why do you think this happened?
2. Why do you think the crystals were different colours?
3. How is the way we formed our crystals similar/different to how they are formed in the Earth's crust?

HOMEWORK:
The students can research a particular type of crystal including how it is formed and its properties.

EXPERIMENT 59

Modelling:
Can we build our own volcano?

LEARNING OBJECTIVES:
Make a model volcanic eruption using a reaction between an acid and an alkali.

INTRODUCTION:
The students create a model volcano and simulate an eruption by reacting bicarbonate of soda with vinegar.

USEFUL PRIOR WORK:
The students should understand the terms acid and alkali.

BACKGROUND SCIENCE:
A volcano is a geological feature formed when a land mass has a vent that goes down into the Earth's crust. At the bottom of the vent is magma (a hot fluid material). When a volcano erupts this magma is ejected from the volcano along with gases and volcanic ash. When magma has erupted from the volcano it is referred to as lava. This lava will eventually cool and form igneous rocks. Volcanoes can be classified as active (erupts on a regular basis), dormant (has not erupted for some time but is expected to erupt again in the future) or extinct (no longer expected to erupt again). A model of a volcano can be made by reacting an acid with an alkali. A good choice is bicarbonate of soda and vinegar. When these substances are reacted they produce a large amount of carbon dioxide gas. This build up of gas is what causes the volcano to erupt. Red food colouring can be added to make the resulting eruption look more like lava.

NATIONAL CURRICULUM LINKS:

Chemical reactions
- chemical reactions as the rearrangement of atoms
- representing chemical reactions using formulae and using equations
- reactions of acids with alkalis to produce a salt plus water.

MATERIALS NEEDED:
Small plastic bottles (for example, water bottles), modelling clay, beakers, funnels, measuring spoons, pipettes, bicarbonate of soda, vinegar, red food colouring, washing-up liquid.

SAFETY AND TECHNICAL NOTES:
- The students can make the body of their volcano from modelling clay. The models could be based on real volcanoes and could be made in advance of the actual experiment.
- Make sure the plastic bottles have been cleaned.
- This investigation can produce a lot of mess so you may want to perform it outside or in a sink.

METHOD:

To be done in advance by the teacher

Have some information and photographs of famous volcanoes for the students to base their models on.

STUDENTS:

1 Build your model volcano using the materials you have been given. Build the model around the plastic bottle. Make sure you do not cover the top of the bottle.
2 Fill the bottle with warm water from the hot tap using a funnel. You want the bottle to be about 3/4 full.
3 Add a few drops of red food colouring and a few drops of washing-up liquid to the bottle using a pipette.
4 Add two teaspoons of bicarbonate of soda to the bottle.
5 When you are ready to have your volcano erupt: place the volcano on a flat surface. Slowly pour vinegar into the plastic bottle until the volcano erupts.

DATA COLLECTION IDEAS:

The students can film their volcanoes erupting.

DIFFERENTIATION:

- **Decrease the challenge:** The students can be helped with measuring out the ingredients.
- **Increase the challenge:** The students can also perform a fair-test style investigation into the quantity of bicarbonate of soda and vinegar used and what effect this has on the eruption.

USEFUL QUESTIONS TO ASK THE STUDENTS:

1 What caused our volcano to erupt?
2 How would changing the quantity of bicarbonate of soda and vinegar used change the eruption?
3 Why do you think we added washing-up liquid to the volcano?

HOMEWORK:

The students could research famous volcanic eruptions, for example Pompeii.

EXPERIMENT 60

Modelling:
How can cabbage be an indicator?

LEARNING OBJECTIVES:
Make our own indicator using red cabbage and test substances to identify whether they are acidic, alkaline or neutral.

INTRODUCTION:
The students use red cabbage to make an indicator and use this to test common household substances.

USEFUL PRIOR WORK:
The students should know what acids, alkalis and indicators are.

BACKGROUND SCIENCE:
Acids and alkalis are two categories of substances based on the concentration of hydrogen ions in the substance. Acids have high concentrations of hydrogen ions, whilst alkalis have low concentrations of hydrogen ions. The strength of acids and alkalis is measured using the pH scale, which runs from one to 14. Acids have a pH of one to six, neutral substances have a pH of seven and alkalis have a pH of eight to 14. The strongest acids have a pH of one and the strongest alkalis have a pH of 14. We can test whether a substance is acidic, neutral or alkaline by using an indicator. An indicator will change colour depending on whether it is in contact with an acid or alkali. Red cabbage contains a purple substance called anthocyanin that acts as an indicator. It will turn pink in an acid, remain purple in a neutral substance and turn blue in an alkali.

NATIONAL CURRICULUM LINKS:

Chemical reactions
- the pH scale for measuring acidity/alkalinity; and indicators.

MATERIALS NEEDED:
Red cabbage, bowls, beakers, stirring rods, teat-pipettes, a selection of common household substances to test, for example: toothpaste, liquid soap, lemon juice, vinegar, orange juice, lemonade, cola, milk, baking soda, water, indigestion tablets, mild kitchen cleaner and cooking oil.

SAFETY AND TECHNICAL NOTES:
- Allow enough time before the start of the investigation for the boiled water to cool.
- Remind the students not to consume any of the food items.
- The red cabbage can stain clothes and skin.
- Do not use any substances that may be harmful to health if consumed or spilt, for example bleach.

METHOD:

To be done in advance by the teacher
Chop up the red cabbage and place it in the bowl. Cover with boiling water.

124 *How can cabbage be an indicator?*

STUDENTS:

1. Set up a row of beakers. You will need one beaker for each substance you will be testing.
2. Add a small amount of the substance you will be testing to each beaker. Use a new teat-pipette for each substance to avoid cross contamination.
3. Collect some of the red cabbage indicator in a beaker. You only need the purple coloured water.
4. Add a few drops of the red cabbage indicator to each beaker using a teat-pipette. Swirl the beaker around for a few seconds. If the substance you are testing has a thicker consistency then it can be helpful to stir it using a stirring rod.
5. Record the colour of the indicator in the results table.

DATA COLLECTION IDEAS:

Substance	Colour of cabbage indicator	Acid or alkali?

DIFFERENTIATION:
- **Decrease the challenge:** The students can be given colour charts to help them identify when the indicator has changed colour.
- **Increase the challenge:** The students could try to make a neutral substance by mixing a known acid and known alkali together (make sure their choices are safe). They can then test the substance using the indicator.

USEFUL QUESTIONS TO ASK THE STUDENTS:

1. Which substances were acidic/alkaline/neutral? Were you surprised by any of your results?
2. Are there any similarities between the types of substances that are acids/alkalis? Why do you think this is?
3. Are there any limitations with testing for acids and alkalis using this method? How could we improve the investigation?

HOMEWORK:

The students can be challenged to find five more common substances that are acidic/alkaline/neutral.

EXPERIMENT 61

Modelling: Can we make a bouncing custard ball?

LEARNING OBJECTIVES:
Make a bouncing custard ball.

INTRODUCTION:
The students use borax, PVA glue and custard powder to make a bouncy ball.

USEFUL PRIOR WORK:
The students should know the particle model for states of matter.

BACKGROUND SCIENCE:
Small, bouncy balls are usually made from an elastic type material such as rubber or certain plastics. These materials are called polymers as they are made up of many small repeating sub-units called monomers. These monomers form long chains that can be stretched or compressed if force is applied to them. This property is what allows bouncy balls to 'bounce'. In this investigation, a polymer is formed from PVA glue reacting with borax. The PVA glue forms cross-links, which create long chains of PVA glue. Custard powder contains cornstarch that holds these cross-links in place (it will also make the balls yellow in colour). The balls formed from this investigation will vary in bounciness depending on the quantities of borax and PVA glue used.

NATIONAL CURRICULUM LINKS:

Materials
- properties of ceramics, polymers and composites (qualitative).

MATERIALS NEEDED:
Borax, PVA glue, custard powder, beakers, bowls, measuring spoons, stirring rods, plastic sandwich bags, non-latex gloves.

SAFETY AND TECHNICAL NOTES:
- The students should wear gloves for this investigation.
- The balls will need to be kept in a sealed plastic bag after they are made or they will dry out and lose their bounciness.

METHOD:

To be done in advance by the teacher
This investigation can be messy so you may want to cover any work surfaces that will be used.

STUDENTS:

1. Add eight tablespoons of warm water from the hot tap into a beaker.
2. Add six tablespoons of custard powder and one teaspoon of borax to the water in the beaker. Stir using a stirring rod.
3. Add one tablespoon of PVA glue into a different beaker.
4. Pour the water mixture into the glue slowly. Stir the mixture with a stirring rod as you pour. Keep stirring the mixture until it forms a solid clump.
5. Take the clump out of the beaker and roll it in your hands until it forms a smooth ball. Try bouncing your ball. If the ball is too wet, try adding some more borax. If the ball is too stiff, try adding some more PVA glue.
6. Test how high your ball will bounce and how many times it will bounce before coming to a stop.
7. Store your bouncy ball in a plastic bag to stop it drying out.

DATA COLLECTION IDEAS:

The students can test how high or how many times their balls bounce. They could also produce illustrated instructions on how to produce a bouncy custard ball.

DIFFERENTIATION:

- **Decrease the challenge:** The students can have the ingredients measured out for them.
- **Increase the challenge:** The students could make a range of balls using different amounts of borax and PVA glue and compare how well they bounce.

USEFUL QUESTIONS TO ASK THE STUDENTS:

1. Why do you think the ball you made is able to bounce?
2. Do you think you would be able to make a much larger bouncing ball using the same method? Why do you think this?
3. In what ways are the bouncy custard balls similar and different to a rubber ball?

HOMEWORK:

The students can research rubber, including where it comes from, and the similarities and differences between natural and synthetic rubber.

EXPERIMENT 62

Observation: How many colours are there in light?

LEARNING OBJECTIVES:
Observe the different colours that make up light.

INTRODUCTION:
The students use a prism to split light into the seven colours of the spectrum.

USEFUL PRIOR WORK:
The students should know that light travels in a straight line.

BACKGROUND SCIENCE:
Visible light (sometimes called white light) is actually made up of seven different colours of light. These colours, red, orange, yellow, green, blue, indigo and violet, are referred to as the spectrum of light. The different colours of light have different wavelengths, with red having the longest wavelength and violet having the shortest wavelength. This means that the different colours of light can be split, or dispersed, by using a prism. Visible light will travel through the air into the prism and then from the prism back into the air. As the light changes the medium through which it is travelling, its speed also changes, and this change in speed causes the light to be refracted. As the degree to which light is refracted is dependent on the wavelength of the light, the different colours in the spectrum will leave the prism at different angles. This will allow the colours of the spectrum to separate and become visible.

NATIONAL CURRICULUM LINKS:

Light
- colours and the different frequencies of light, white light and prisms (qualitative only); differential colour effects in absorption and diffuse reflection.

MATERIALS NEEDED:
Prisms, light boxes with one slit, white paper, coloured filters.

SAFETY AND TECHNICAL NOTES:
- The colours of the spectrum may be difficult to see, so performing this investigation in a slightly darkened room may help the students.
- The bulbs in the light boxes can become hot after prolonged use.

METHOD:

To be done in advance by the teacher
Reduce the amount of light in the room by drawing blinds and turning off unnecessary lights. Make sure the room is still light enough for the students to move around safely.

STUDENTS:

1 Place a ray box onto a piece of white card. The white card will help you to see the different colours in the spectrum.
2 Make sure you have just one ray of light coming from the ray box. You should be able to see the ray of light on the card.
3 Place a prism onto the card so that the ray of light passes through the prism. Adjust the prism and ray box until you are able to see the colours of the spectrum on the card.
4 Use a second prism to see if you can put the colours of the spectrum back together again so you have one ray of visible light passing out of the second prism.
5 Remove the second prism and place a coloured filter in the path of the light coming out of the prism. What do you observe? Do the same with the other coloured filters.

DATA COLLECTION IDEAS:

The students can draw what they observe for each part of the investigation. For more detailed results the students could use a protractor to measure the angle of each colour in the spectrum.

DIFFERENTIATION:

- **Decrease the challenge:** The students may need help adjusting the prism so that the spectrum is visible.
- **Increase the challenge:** The students could measure the minimum and maximum angle that the light can enter the prism for all or some of the spectrum to be visible.

USEFUL QUESTIONS TO ASK THE STUDENTS:

1 What were you able to observe as the light passed through the prism/s? Why do you think this happened?
2 What happened when you used the coloured filters? Why do you think this happened?
3 How do you think rainbows in the sky are formed?

HOMEWORK:

The students can research other uses of prisms, for example in optical instruments and in ophthalmology.

EXPERIMENT 63

Observation: How does pressure vary in a water column?

LEARNING OBJECTIVES:
Observe how water moves out of a container through different holes.

INTRODUCTION:
The students use metal tins with holes placed in different locations in order to observe how water moves out of the tin.

USEFUL PRIOR WORK:
The students should be familiar with the term pressure.

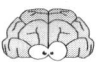

BACKGROUND SCIENCE:
Pressure is the amount of force exerted by a liquid or gas over a particular area. Liquids and gases do not have fixed shapes, which means that they will take the shape of their container. In terms of liquids, the pressure at the bottom of the container will be greater than the pressure at the top of the container due to the weight of the liquid pushing downwards. This principle can be demonstrated using a tin can with holes punched into the sides of the tin. If the holes are at the top of the tin then the water will just dribble out of the holes with very little force. However, if the holes are at the bottom of the tin then the water will spurt out of the tin with a high level of force due to the increased pressure of the water at the bottom of the tin. For a tin with an irregular shape it can be shown that the water will leave the tin at right angles to the hole, demonstrating that pressure acts in all directions. The size of the holes can also affect how the water leaves the tin due to Bernoulli's Principle. Bernoulli discovered that a liquid has a lower pressure when it is moving faster, therefore water will leave a tin more quickly through smaller holes.

NATIONAL CURRICULUM LINKS:

Forces:
- pressure in liquids, increasing with depth; upthrust effects, floating and sinking
- pressure measured by ratio of force over area – acting normal to any surface.

MATERIALS NEEDED:
Empty metal tins (for example, baked bean tins), jugs or large beakers, water.

SAFETY AND TECHNICAL NOTES:
- Each group will require three tins. One tin where three holes have been drilled on the same level around the tin, one tin where three holes have been drilled with one at the top, one in the middle and one at the bottom of the tin, and one tin that has been slightly deformed (this can be achieved by denting the tin using a hammer) and has three holes drilled on the same level around the tin.
- Ensure any tins that contained food have been cleaned.
- You may want to carry out this investigation in a sink or in a tray in order to collect the water.
- Using ring-pull style tins will reduce the chance of sharp edges on the tins.

METHOD:

To be done in advance by the teacher
Ensure the tins have been prepared and cleaned.

STUDENTS:

1 Select the tin that has three holes all on the same level. Place the tin into a sink or tray.
2 Fill a jug with water. Pour the water into the tin so that the tin fills with water but does not come over the top of the tin. Keep pouring the water into the tin as the water leaves the tin through the holes. Observe how the water leaves through the holes.
3 Repeat the investigation for the other two tins.

DATA COLLECTION IDEAS:
The students can draw diagrams showing how the water leaves the tin for each investigation.

DIFFERENTIATION:
- **Decrease the challenge:** The students could use a video camera to record what happens then they can watch it back in slow motion.
- **Increase the challenge:** The students can test a larger range of holes including coming up with their own arrangements of holes. These could be tested using polystyrene cups with the holes made using a pin.

USEFUL QUESTIONS TO ASK THE STUDENTS:
1 What did you observe as the water left each of the tins? Why do you think this happened?
2 What do you think would happen if we used holes that were different sizes?
3 Do you think gases would leave the tins in the same way as liquids? Why do you think this?

HOMEWORK:
The students can investigate water pressure in seas and oceans and why it is important for divers to descend and ascend gradually.

EXPERIMENT 64

Observation:
What do waves look like?

LEARNING OBJECTIVES:
Observe how waves travel through water.

INTRODUCTION:
The students observe the frequency and wavelength of waves in a ripple tank.

USEFUL PRIOR WORK:
The students should know the names of the different parts of a wave.

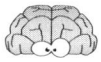

BACKGROUND SCIENCE:
Waves are caused by energy being transferred via vibrations. In waves only energy, and not matter, is being transferred. There are two different types of wave, longitudinal waves and transverse waves. In longitudinal waves, the observed vibrations are in the same direction the wave is travelling. In transverse waves, the observed vibrations are at right angles to the direction the wave is travelling. Waves travelling through water are examples of transverse waves. The different parts of a wave have specific names. The highest point of a wave is called the peak and the lowest point is called the trough. The distance between two peaks or two troughs is called the wavelength of the wave. The frequency of a wave is the number of waves passing a particular point in a certain amount of time.

NATIONAL CURRICULUM LINKS:

Observed waves
- waves on water as undulations that travel through water with transverse motion; these waves can be reflected, and add or cancel – superposition.

MATERIALS NEEDED:
Ripple tank and accessories, power supplies, rulers, large pieces of white card.

SAFETY AND TECHNICAL NOTES:
- Performing this investigation in a slightly darkened room may help the students see the waves.

METHOD:

To be done in advance by the teacher
Set up the ripple tanks if the students will not be doing this themselves. Reduce the light levels in the room. Ensure the room is still light enough for the students to move around safely.

STUDENTS:

1. Place the ripple tank on a stable, flat surface with a piece of white card underneath. Connect up the power supply.
2. Pour enough water into the tank to come up to a depth of about 1/2cm.
3. Lower the wooden rod so that it touches the surface of the water.

4 Turn on the lamp and the motor. Adjust the lamp until you can see the pattern of the waves on the card. Make notes on what you observe.
5 Count how many waves pass a particular point in 10 seconds. Divide this number by 10 to calculate the frequency of the waves. Record your result.
6 Use the ruler to measure the wavelength of one of the waves. Remember to measure from a peak to a peak or a trough to a trough. Record your result.

DATA COLLECTION IDEAS:
The students can draw their observations and record any measurements they take.

DIFFERENTIATION:
- **Decrease the challenge:** The students may need help with measuring the wavelength of the waves.
- **Increase the challenge:** The students can use the wavelength and the frequency to calculate the speed of the waves.

USEFUL QUESTIONS TO ASK THE STUDENTS:
1 What did you observe about the waves and how they travelled through the water?
2 What do you think would happen if we increased the power to the motor? Why do you think this?
3 How do you think waves on beaches might differ from the ones we observe in ripple tanks? Why do you think this?

HOMEWORK:
The students can research tsunamis and how they are formed.

EXPERIMENT 65

Observation: Which objects will give you a static shock?

LEARNING OBJECTIVES:
Observe which materials produce static electricity.

INTRODUCTION:
The students observe the static electricity produced by different materials.

USEFUL PRIOR WORK:
The students should understand the term static electricity.

BACKGROUND SCIENCE:
Static electricity occurs when electrically charged particles form on the surface of an object. This can be caused by two objects rubbing against each other, an object that is able to give up electrons easily and an object that is able to gain electrons easily, causing electrons to build up on the surface of one of the objects. These electrically charged particles will remain on the surface of the object until they have been discharged by coming into contact with another surface. This discharge can be quick, resulting in a static electric shock. Static electricity can also cause two objects to become attracted to each other (a positively charged object and a negatively charged object). For example, a balloon that is statically charged will be able to attract small pieces of paper (an example of a positively charged object) until the negative charge of the balloon is discharged by coming into contact with a grounded object.

NATIONAL CURRICULUM LINKS:

Static electricity
- separation of positive or negative charges when objects are rubbed together: transfer of electrons, forces between charged objects
- the idea of electric field, forces acting across the space between objects not in contact.

MATERIALS NEEDED:
Balloons, polyester cloth, cotton cloth, wool cloth, silk cloth, nylon cloth, tracing paper, plastic wrap, anti-static cloth, paper cut up into small pieces, white tile.

SAFETY AND TECHNICAL NOTES:
- Ensure that the pieces of cloth used are a similar size.

METHOD:

To be done in advance by the teacher
Cut a sheet of paper up into small pieces if the students will not be doing this themselves. Inflate the balloons if the students will not be doing this themselves.

STUDENTS:

1 Place the pieces of white paper onto a white tile.
2 Take a balloon and rub the balloon 10 times onto your hair.
3 Hold the balloon over the pieces of paper and observe what happens. Record your observations.
4 Discharge the balloon by touching it on a grounded object, for example a radiator.
5 Repeat the investigation by rubbing the balloon onto the different materials you are testing. Remember to discharge the balloon between each material.

DATA COLLECTION IDEAS:
The students can write down their observations for the different materials.

DIFFERENTIATION:
- **Decrease the challenge:** The students can test a smaller number of materials to give them time to observe what happens in the investigation.
- **Increase the challenge:** The students can use this investigation as the basis for planning and conducting a fair-test style investigation into static electricity.

USEFUL QUESTIONS TO ASK THE STUDENTS:
1 What did you observe when you tested each of the materials? Did any of your results surprise you?
2 Why do you think the paper was attracted to the balloon?
3 Can you think of any situations where static electricity might be useful or dangerous?

HOMEWORK:
The students can research how photocopiers use static electricity to produce photocopies.

EXPERIMENT 66

Observation: How do gases move?

LEARNING OBJECTIVES:
Observe how the particles in a gas move.

INTRODUCTION:
The students observe Brownian motion using a smoke cell.

USEFUL PRIOR WORK:
The students should be familiar with the particle model of matter.

BACKGROUND SCIENCE:
Brownian motion refers to the random motion of particles in a gas or liquid. It is named after the scientist Robert Brown who discovered the phenomenon in 1827 while observing particles under a microscope. The most common way to observe Brownian motion is to use a smoke cell. This consists of a glass cell, a lamp and a lens placed onto the stage of a microscope. A small amount of smoke is released into the cell allowing the students to observe the movements of the particles using the microscope. The smoke particles will appear to move around in a jittery motion. This is because the smoke particles are randomly hitting invisible air molecules. This causes the smoke particles to move but, as the air molecules cannot be seen, it appears as if the smoke particles are moving randomly by themselves. Smoke is used in this investigation as it is easy for the students to see down the microscope.

NATIONAL CURRICULUM LINKS:

Matter
- Brownian motion in gases.

MATERIALS NEEDED:
Smoke cell with a light and lens, microscope, microscope cover slip, power pack, smoke source.

SAFETY AND TECHNICAL NOTES:
- The smoke source can come from a burning paper straw. Light the straw at one end and then extinguish the flame so that it remains smoking.

METHOD:

To be done in advance by the teacher
Prepare the smoke cells the students will be using. Fill the cells with smoke if the students will not be doing this themselves.

STUDENTS:

1 Set up the smoke cell on the microscope stage. Connect the smoke cell to a power source.
2 Use the lens with the lowest level of magnification first. Observe the smoke cell. Make notes and diagrams on what you can see.

136 *How do gases move?*

✏ DATA COLLECTION IDEAS:
The students can draw a series of diagrams of what they observe.

DIFFERENTIATION:
- **Decrease the challenge:** The microscope can be connected to a visualiser so the movements can be observed by the whole class on a whiteboard.
- **Increase the challenge:** The students can compare Brownian motion in gases with Brownian motion in liquids by observing small particles suspended in a liquid under a microscope.

USEFUL QUESTIONS TO ASK THE STUDENTS:
1. What did you observe under the microscope? Why do you think this happened?
2. Do you think Brownian motion would occur in liquids? Why do you think this?
3. How does Brownian motion help us to understand the structure of atoms and molecules?

HOMEWORK:
The students can research Robert Brown and how he discovered Brownian motion.

EXPERIMENT 67

Observation: How much 'stuff' do we make in a reaction?

LEARNING OBJECTIVES:
Observe what happens to the mass of reactants and products in a reaction.

INTRODUCTION:
The students react potassium iodide and lead nitrate in order to show that there is no change in mass following the reaction.

USEFUL PRIOR WORK:
The students should understand the term mass.

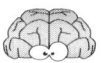

BACKGROUND SCIENCE:
Atoms are the basic building blocks of everything in the universe. Atoms consist of an inner nucleus that contains positively charged protons and neutrally charged neutrons. Around the outside of the nucleus are electron shells that hold negatively charged electrons. The mass of the atom is the total number of protons and neutrons in the nucleus. During a chemical reaction, no atoms are created or destroyed; rather, they are simply re-arranged into different products. This means that no mass is lost or gained during a chemical reaction. This is the conservation of mass principle – the total mass of the reactants is always equal to the total mass of the products. It is possible to observe some very small differences in mass when carrying out reactions in school-based investigations due to human error and the sensitivity of the equipment being used.

NATIONAL CURRICULUM LINKS:

Physical changes
- conservation of material and of mass, and reversibility, in melting, freezing, evaporation, sublimation, condensation, dissolving.

MATERIALS NEEDED:
Beakers, measuring cylinders, balance, potassium iodide solution, lead nitrate solution, eye protection.

SAFETY AND TECHNICAL NOTES:
- Eye protection should be worn for this investigation.
- The students should wash their hands after this investigation.

METHOD:

To be done in advance by the teacher
Ensure there are enough balances available in the room so the students do not have to wait a long time to measure their beakers.

STUDENTS:

1. Use a measuring cylinder to add 5cm³ of potassium iodide to a beaker.
2. Use a new measuring cylinder to add 5cm³ of lead nitrate to another beaker.
3. Use the balance to measure the total mass of both of the beakers. Record this result.
4. Carefully pour the contents of one beaker into the other beaker. Make sure you get all of the contents of the beaker into the other beaker.
5. Use the balance to measure the total mass of both of the beakers again. Record the result.

DATA COLLECTION IDEAS:

The students can make notes on the mass of the substances and any observations they make during the reaction.

DIFFERENTIATION:

- **Decrease the challenge:** The reactants could be measured out in advance for the students to use.
- **Increase the challenge:** The students can carry out further conservation of mass reactions and compare how accurate their measurements are.

USEFUL QUESTIONS TO ASK THE STUDENTS:

1. What happened to the mass of the substances before and after the reaction? Why do you think this happened?
2. Why might there be some small changes of mass observed in reactions?
3. Why is it important to take very accurate measurements when conducting science experiments?

HOMEWORK:

The students can calculate the mass of some chemical compounds such as water and sodium chloride using the periodic table.

EXPERIMENT 68

Fair testing: How can we change the brightness of a bulb?

LEARNING OBJECTIVES:
Investigate how dimmer switches control the brightness of a bulb.

INTRODUCTION:
The students use different lengths of resistance wire to investigate the effect on the brightness of a bulb in an electrical circuit.

USEFUL PRIOR WORK:
The students should be able to construct an electrical circuit.

BACKGROUND SCIENCE:
A dimmer switch is an example of a variable resistor. It allows the brightness of a bulb to be controlled rather than just simply being turned on or off. A resistor is anything that resists the flow of electrical current around an electrical circuit. Most electrical components, including light bulbs, will produce some resistance but a variable resistor allows the amount of resistance produced to be controlled by the user. In terms of a dimmer switch for a light, the light will become dimmer as the resistance in the electrical circuit is increased and brighter as the resistance in the electrical circuit is decreased. The resistance is controlled by altering the length of material that the electrical current has to travel through. The longer the length of the material, the greater the resistance.

NATIONAL CURRICULUM LINKS:

Electricity and electromagnetism
- electric current, measured in amperes, in circuits, series and parallel circuits, currents add where branches meet and current as flow of charge
- potential difference, measured in volts, battery and bulb ratings; resistance, measured in ohms, as the ratio of potential difference (p.d.) to current.

MATERIALS NEEDED:
1.5V cells, cell holders, connecting wires, bulbs in bulb holder, crocodile clips, resistance wire, rulers, tracing paper.

SAFETY AND TECHNICAL NOTES:
- Remind students to switch their circuits off when they are not being tested.
- Bulbs can become hot after prolonged use.
- The dimly lit bulbs may be difficult to see, so performing this investigation in a slightly darkened room may help the students.

How to change the brightness of a bulb

METHOD:

To be done in advance by the teacher
Reduce the amount of light in the room by drawing blinds and turning off unnecessary lights. Make sure the room is still light enough for the students to move around safely. Cut up pieces of tracing paper for the students to use in the investigation. Approximately 1/8th of an A4-sized piece of paper will be sufficient.

STUDENTS:

1. Set up a simple circuit using the cells, bulbs and connecting wires. Leave a gap in the circuit.
2. Use a ruler to measure the length of resistance wire that you will be testing first and place a crocodile clip and connecting wire at each end. You do not need to cut the wire.
3. Place the resistance wire into the gap in your circuit. Hold the tracing paper over the bulb in the circuit. Keep adding another piece of tracing paper until you can no longer see the light from the bulb through the paper. Record how many pieces of tracing paper it took to block the light.
4. Repeat the investigation with the rest of the lengths of resistance wire that you are testing.

DATA COLLECTION IDEAS:

Length of resistance wire (mm)	No. of sheets of tracing paper needed to block the light

DIFFERENTIATION:
- **Decrease the challenge:** The different lengths of resistance wire can be made for the students by cutting the wire and sticking it to a piece of card.
- **Increase the challenge:** The students can be challenged to design a dimmer switch.

USEFUL QUESTIONS TO ASK THE STUDENTS:
1. What happened when you decreased/increased the length of the resistance wire? Why do you think this happened?
2. How could you use this information to produce a dimmer switch for a light?
3. What other electrical devices could we control in a similar way?

HOMEWORK:
The students can investigate how other types of switch work, for example tilt switches and LED switches.

EXPERIMENT 69

Fair testing: Why do moon craters vary in size?

LEARNING OBJECTIVES:
Investigate how the height a meteorite falls from affects the size of the resulting moon crater.

INTRODUCTION:
The students investigate how the height of a meteorite impacts the size of the resulting moon crater by dropping a marble into a tray of sand.

USEFUL PRIOR WORK:
The students should know what moon craters are and how they are formed.

BACKGROUND SCIENCE:
The moon has a large number of craters covering its surface. These craters are caused by other space objects, such as meteorites, crashing into the surface of the moon. They leave behind a bowl-shaped hole surrounded by a raised ring. The moon has so many craters because, unlike the Earth, it does not have an atmosphere. This means that incoming meteors cannot be burnt up before they reach the surface of the moon. The craters on the moon are not identical however, with some craters being much wider and deeper than other craters. This is due to the amount of kinetic energy the object has when it hits the surface of the moon. Kinetic energy is determined by an object's mass and speed – the greater the mass and speed, the greater the kinetic energy and the larger the resulting crater. The angle of impact also has an effect on the size of the crater.

NATIONAL CURRICULUM LINKS:

Space physics
- gravity force, weight = mass × gravitational field strength (g), on Earth g = 10 N/kg, different on other planets and stars; gravity forces between Earth and Moon, and between Earth and Sun (qualitative only).

MATERIALS NEEDED:
Marbles, small tray or dish filled with sand, metre ruler, 30cm ruler, forceps (optional), timer (optional).

SAFETY AND TECHNICAL NOTES:
- Ensure the trays are filled with at least 5cm of sand.

METHOD:

To be done in advance by the teacher
Prepare the trays of sand if this will not be done by the students.

STUDENTS:

1 Gently shake your tray of sand to ensure it is evenly distributed and that there is a smooth surface.

Why do moon craters vary in size?

2 Hold the marble above the tray of sand. Select the first height you will be testing. Use the ruler to check the height you are dropping it from. Aim to drop the marble in the centre of the tray of sand. Let go of the marble.
3 Carefully remove the marble without disturbing the crater it has left behind. You may find it easier to remove the marble using forceps.
4 Use a ruler to measure the diameter of the crater. Record this in your table.
5 Smooth over the sand again and repeat the investigation two more times for that height.
6 Repeat the investigation for the rest of the heights.

DATA COLLECTION IDEAS:

Height marble dropped from (cm)	Diameter of crater (mm)			
	Trial 1	Trial 2	Trial 3	Average

DIFFERENTIATION:
- **Decrease the challenge:** The students may find it easier to measure the crater while the marble is still in the sand.
- **Increase the challenge:** The students could attempt to calculate the speed of each meteor by also recording the time taken for the marble to hit the tray of sand.

USEFUL QUESTIONS TO ASK THE STUDENTS:
1 What effect did changing the height you dropped the marble from have on the size of the crater? Why do you think this happened?
2 What other factors might affect the size of a crater?
3 Why do you think the Earth has fewer visible craters than the moon?

HOMEWORK:
The students can produce a graph of their results.

EXPERIMENT 70

Fair testing: What are the most dangerous weather conditions to drive in?

LEARNING OBJECTIVES:
Investigate the effect of different types of weather on how quickly a car travels down a slope.

INTRODUCTION:
The students use blocks of wood to simulate different driving conditions in order to see how quickly a toy car will travel down a ramp.

USEFUL PRIOR WORK:
The students should know what friction is and its effects.

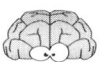

BACKGROUND SCIENCE:
Friction is a type of force that occurs when two surfaces rub against each other. Friction will typically act in the opposite direction of motion, meaning that friction will act to slow down objects. Sometimes friction is a useful force, for example the friction between a car's tyres and the road allow the car to grip onto the road and travel along it in a controlled manner. The strength of the force of friction is determined by the coefficient of friction (how much the two moving objects are coming into contact with each other) and the mass of the moving objects (the greater the mass, the greater the force of friction). If a car is travelling down a road where the coefficient of friction is very low, for example on an icy road, then the force of friction will be very low. This will make it hard for the tyres of the car to grip onto the road, making it more difficult to control the car.

NATIONAL CURRICULUM LINKS:

Forces
- Forces associated with deforming objects; stretching and squashing – springs; with rubbing and friction between surfaces, with pushing things out of the way; resistance to motion of air and water.

MATERIALS NEEDED:
Wooden boards suitable for building a ramp, toy cars, timers or data-loggers with light gates.

SAFETY AND TECHNICAL NOTES:
- Use wooden boards that have been soaked in water to represent the wet roads.
- Use wooden boards that have been soaked in water and then left in the freezer to represent the icy roads. Leave the icy boards in the freezer until they are needed.

METHOD:

To be done in advance by the teacher
Prepare the 'icy' roads by soaking the wooden boards in water and then leaving them to freeze overnight.

STUDENTS:

1. Assemble your ramp using a dry wooden board. This board will represent driving on a dry road. Place your car at the top of the ramp. Let go of the car and start the timer. Stop the timer when the car reaches the end of the ramp. Repeat this two more times. Record your results in your results table and calculate an average.
2. Remove the dry wooden board and replace with a wet wooden board. This board will represent driving on a wet road. Repeat the investigation using the wet wooden board.
3. Remove the wet wooden board and replace with an icy wooden board. This board will represent driving on an icy road. Repeat the investigation using the icy wooden board.
4. Keep using the icy wooden board but sprinkle the board with a handful of sand. This board will represent driving on an icy road that has been gritted. Repeat the investigation using the icy wooden board.

DATA COLLECTION IDEAS:

Condition of road	Time taken for a car to reach the end of the ramp (s)			
	Trial 1	Trial 2	Trial 3	Average

DIFFERENTIATION:
- **Decrease the challenge:** The students can work in small groups with each group investigating one driving condition. The results can then be pooled at the end of the investigation.
- **Increase the challenge:** The students can attempt to calculate the speed the car is travelling down the ramp.

USEFUL QUESTIONS TO ASK THE STUDENTS:
1. Which driving conditions were the least/most dangerous? Why do you think this was?
2. What could be done to make dangerous road conditions safer?
3. What other factors could affect how quickly a car could stop in an emergency?

HOMEWORK:
The students could research stopping distances for cars travelling at different speeds.

EXPERIMENT 71

Fair testing: How can we increase the resistance in a circuit?

LEARNING OBJECTIVES:
Investigating how the thickness of a wire affects its resistance in an electrical circuit.

INTRODUCTION:
The students investigate how the resistance of a piece of wire changes as its diameter is changed.

USEFUL PRIOR WORK:
The students should be able to build simple, electrical circuits.

BACKGROUND SCIENCE:
Resistance refers to how much a component in an electrical circuit resists the flow of the electric current. A component with a high resistance will make it harder for the electric current to flow through the circuit. The unit for measuring resistance is ohms. An electrical current is the flow of negatively charged electrons through a conducting material. As the electrons pass through a metal such as a wire they are likely to collide with the atoms that make up the metal. If the wire is longer the resistance will be greater because there are more atoms present for the electrons to collide with. If the wire is thinner the resistance will be greater as there is less space for the current to flow through the wire.

NATIONAL CURRICULUM LINKS:

Current electricity
- electric current, measured in amperes, in circuits, series and parallel circuits, currents add where branches meet and current as flow of charge
- potential difference, measured in volts, battery and bulb ratings; resistance, measured in ohms, as the ratio of potential difference (p.d.) to current.

MATERIALS NEEDED:
Cells and cell holders, ammeters, connecting wires and crocodile clips, resistance wires of different diameters.

SAFETY AND TECHNICAL NOTES:
- Use fine gauge wires to prevent the wires heating up and affecting the results.

METHOD:

To be done in advance by the teacher
Ensure the different wires are labelled with their diameters.

STUDENTS:

1. Build a simple series circuit using the cells, ammeters and connecting wires.
2. Make a gap in the circuit and add the first piece of wire you will be testing.
3. Record the reading on the ammeter in your results table.
4. Repeat the investigation with the rest of the wires you will be testing.

DATA COLLECTION IDEAS:

Diameter of resistance wire (mm)	Current in the circuit (A)

DIFFERENTIATION:

- **Decrease the challenge:** The electrical circuits can be premade for the students on cork boards so they only have to add the wire to the circuit.
- **Increase the challenge:** The students can also investigate how the length of the wire affects the resistance.

USEFUL QUESTIONS TO ASK THE STUDENTS:

1. What happened to the resistance of the wire as the diameter increased? Why do you think this happened?
2. What do you think would happen if we used wires that were different lengths? Why do you think this?
3. Why is this information useful to people that design electrical devices?

HOMEWORK:

The students can research the known resistance of a selection of different metals.

EXPERIMENT 72

Fair testing: How can blood spatter solve a crime?

LEARNING OBJECTIVES:
Investigate how the height a blood drop falls from affects its diameter.

INTRODUCTION:
The students simulate blood spatter patterns by dropping fake blood from different heights and then measuring the diameter of the resulting blood spatter.

USEFUL PRIOR WORK:
The students should be familiar with forces and gravity.

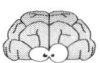

BACKGROUND SCIENCE:
Blood spatter analysis is a specialised area of forensic science that deals with blood stains left behind at a crime scene. These bloodstains can provide useful information to the people investigating the crime such as how someone was attacked, what they were attacked with, the height of the attacker etc. Blood spatter patterns are caused when blood droplets are dispersed through the air. If these droplets come into contact with a surface they will leave behind a distinct pattern based on the height the drop fell from, the angle of the impact that caused the injury and the speed and distance travelled by the blood drop. Measuring the width and length of any bloodstains allows scientists to calculate the height and angle of the original injury.

NATIONAL CURRICULUM LINKS:

Describing motion
- speed and the quantitative relationship between average speed, distance and time (speed = distance ÷ time).

Forces
- non-contact forces: gravity forces acting at a distance on Earth and in space, forces between magnets, and forces due to static electricity.

Forces and motion
- forces being needed to cause objects to stop or start moving, or to change their speed or direction of motion (qualitative only)
- change depending on direction of force and its size.

MATERIALS NEEDED:
Boss and clamp stand, teat-pipettes, rulers, white tiles, timers (optional), fake blood (see safety and technical notes), paper towels.

SAFETY AND TECHNICAL NOTES:
- The fake blood can simply be red food colouring, however mixing red food colouring with a small amount of cornflour will produce a thicker consistency that more closely resembles real blood.

148   *How can blood spatter solve a crime?*

METHOD:

To be done in advance by the teacher
Prepare the fake blood the students will be using (see safety and technical notes).

STUDENTS:

1. Set up a boss and clamp stand. Fill a teat-pipette with the fake blood and place it in the boss so that it points directly downwards.
2. Place a white tile underneath the teat-pipette. Squeeze a practice drop from the teat-pipette to make sure it falls onto the middle of the white tile.
3. Use a ruler to measure the height of the teat-pipette. Measure from the end of the teat-pipette where the blood will be falling from. Set the teat-pipette for the first height you will be testing.
4. Squeeze the teat-pipette gently so that one drop of blood falls onto the white tile. Use a ruler to measure the diameter of the drop on the white tile. Record this in your results table. Wipe the blood drop off the white tile with a paper towel. Repeat for this height two more times. Calculate the average diameter of the drops.
5. Repeat the investigation for the rest of the heights you will be testing.

DATA COLLECTION IDEAS:

Height blood dropped from (cm)	Diameter of blood spatter (mm)			
	Trial 1	Trial 2	Trial 3	Average

DIFFERENTIATION:
- **Decrease the challenge:** The students may need help measuring the diameter of the blood drops.
- **Increase the challenge:** The students could also try to calculate the speed the blood drops are travelling at by using the equation speed = distance/time.

USEFUL QUESTIONS TO ASK THE STUDENTS:
1. What happened to the diameter of the blood drops as the height they fell from increased? Why do you think this happened?
2. Why would this sort of information be useful to people investigating a crime?
3. What do you think would happen if the blood drops fell in windy conditions? How could we test what would happen?

HOMEWORK:
The students could research other types of forensics, for example ballistics or trace evidence.

EXPERIMENT 73

Fair testing: Can we stop radio waves?

LEARNING OBJECTIVES:
Investigate if there are any materials that can block radio waves.

INTRODUCTION:
The students test different materials to see if they are able to block radio waves.

USEFUL PRIOR WORK:
The students should be familiar with waves.

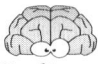

BACKGROUND SCIENCE:
Radio waves are an example of non-harmful electromagnetic radiation. They are most commonly used for communication services. Radio waves require two different components in order to be transmitted: a transmitting antenna that relays the radio signal from a device creating a radio wave and a receiving antenna that picks up the radio waves produced by the transmitting antenna. Whether a radio wave is able to travel through a material is referred to as transmittance. Materials that allow radio waves to travel through are called good transmitters and materials that do not allow radio waves to travel through are called poor transmitters.

NATIONAL CURRICULUM LINKS:

Energy and waves
- pressure waves transferring energy; use for cleaning and physiotherapy by ultrasound; waves transferring information for conversion to electrical signals by microphone.

MATERIALS NEEDED:
A radio controlled device (for example, a car), a selection of materials to test (for example, paper towels, newspaper, aluminium foil, zinc foil, copper foil), cling film, cotton, rubber, plastic bag etc., sellotape.

SAFETY AND TECHNICAL NOTES:
- Some metal foils can be harmful to the environment. Ensure they are not thrown away by the students.

METHOD:

To be done in advance by the teacher
Test the radio-controlled devices to make sure they work. Ensure they have fresh batteries. Have a suitable space prepared for the students to test the radio-controlled devices.

STUDENTS:

1. Test your radio-controlled device. Observe how it moves including how quickly it responds.
2. Cover the controller in the first material you will be testing. Use a small amount of sellotape to hold it in place if necessary.

150   *Can we stop radio waves?*

3 Test the radio-controlled device again. Observe how it responds. Record the results in your results table.
4 Repeat the investigation for the rest of the materials you will be testing.

✎ DATA COLLECTION IDEAS:

Material	Observations

DIFFERENTIATION:
- **Decrease the challenge:** The students can simply test whether the radio-controlled device works.
- **Increase the challenge:** The students could also investigate whether the thickness of the material affects its transmittance by layering up the materials that do allow radio waves to pass through.

USEFUL QUESTIONS TO ASK THE STUDENTS:
1 Which materials allowed the radio waves to pass through? Why do you think they were able to do this?
2 Why is it important to know which materials will allow radio waves to pass through them?
3 Where in everyday life do we use radio waves?

HOMEWORK:
The students can research how radio waves can be transmitted over long distances.

EXPERIMENT 74

Pattern seeking: How can you make a swing go faster?

LEARNING OBJECTIVES:
Investigate how the length of the chain on a swing affects how fast the swing goes.

INTRODUCTION:
The students investigate how altering the length of a swing chain (an example of a pendulum) affects how long the swing takes to complete a period.

USEFUL PRIOR WORK:
The students should know about balanced and unbalanced forces.

BACKGROUND SCIENCE:
A pendulum is an example of a device that can rotate around a fixed point. When a pendulum is released it is able to swing in the direction of the ground due to the force of gravity and then continue swinging due to its inertia. The time it takes for a pendulum to complete a full swing, swinging away from and then back to its original starting position, is called a period. The length of time it takes for a pendulum to complete one period can be affected by different factors. One example is the length of the chain that the pendulum is attached to. The longer the chain, the longer it will take for the pendulum to complete one period. If additional force is applied to the pendulum, rather than just letting go of the pendulum, the time taken to complete one period will be shorter. The mass of the pendulum, however, does not affect the time taken for the period as the force of gravity acts on all objects equally.

NATIONAL CURRICULUM LINKS:

Forces
- forces as pushes or pulls, arising from the interaction between two objects
- using force arrows in diagrams, adding forces in one dimension, balanced and unbalanced forces
- moment as the turning effect of a force.

MATERIALS NEEDED:
Pendulums, boss and clamp stands, timers, rulers, scissors.

SAFETY AND TECHNICAL NOTES:
- Use 30cm as the maximum length of the pendulum.
- Demonstrate that the period the students are measuring is the time taken for the pendulum to swing and then return back to its starting position.
- The pendulum should be released from a 90° angle so that the pendulum swings 180° in total.
- Remind the students that they should let go of the pendulum and not apply any force.

152 *How can you make a swing go faster?*

METHOD:

To be done in advance by the teacher
Prepare the pendulums that the students will be using with an initial length of 30cm.

STUDENTS:

1. Set up a boss and clamp stand at the edge of a table. Attach the pendulum string to the clamp so that it hangs down in front of the pendulum and is able to swing freely.
2. Raise your pendulum to the starting point and then let go of the pendulum. Start the timer when the pendulum released and stop the timer when the pendulum swings back to the starting point. Record the result in your results table. Repeat two more times and record the results in your results table.
3. Remove the pendulum from the clamp stand use a ruler to measure the next length you will be testing. Cut off the excess string and reattach your pendulum. Repeat the investigation.
4. Repeat the investigation with all the lengths that you are testing.

DATA COLLECTION IDEAS:

Length of pendulum string (cm)	Time taken for one period (s)			
	Trial 1	Trial 2	Trial 3	Average

DIFFERENTIATION:
- **Decrease the challenge:** The students may need assisting with timing the length of the period.
- **Increase the challenge:** The students can investigate other factors such as the height the pendulum is released from.

USEFUL QUESTIONS TO ASK THE STUDENTS:
1. Was there any pattern in your results? What do the results tell you?
2. What other factors do you think would affect the time taken for a pendulum to complete one period?
3. What forces are acting on the swing during the period of movement?

HOMEWORK:
The students can draw force diagrams for the pendulum.

EXPERIMENT 75

Pattern seeking: Can you break a spring?

LEARNING OBJECTIVES:
Will a spring always return to its original length?

INTRODUCTION:
The students investigate Hooke's law by adding weights to a spring.

USEFUL PRIOR WORK:
The students should understand the basic principles of forces.

BACKGROUND SCIENCE:
A spring is an object that exhibits the property of elasticity. An elastic object is one that can be deformed, stretched or squashed but will still return to its original shape when the forces acting on it are removed. Springs (and some other elastic objects) will also follow Hooke's law. This law is named after the scientist Robert Hooke who discovered the principle. Hooke's law states that the amount of stretch shown by an object is proportional to the force applied to the object. Therefore, if you double the amount of weight added to the object the amount of stretch shown by the object will also double. Most elastic objects, however, have something called the 'elastic limit'. This is the point at which too much weight has been added to the object and it will no longer return to its original shape. Springs are an example of objects that have an elastic limit.

NATIONAL CURRICULUM LINKS:

Forces
- forces: associated with deforming objects; stretching and squashing – springs; with rubbing and friction between surfaces, with pushing things out of the way; resistance to motion of air and water
- forces measured in newtons, measurements of stretch or compression as force is changed
- force-extension linear relation; Hooke's law as a special case.

MATERIALS NEEDED:
Springs, boss and clamp stands, small weights, weight holder, rulers.

SAFETY AND TECHNICAL NOTES:
- You may want to test the springs before the investigation to find their elastic limit.
- You can decide whether you want the students to only add weights up to this point.
- You could perform a demonstration by adding enough weight to a spring so that it goes beyond its elastic limit.

METHOD:

To be done in advance by the teacher
Test the springs to find their elastic limit (see safety and technical notes).

154 *Can you break a spring?*

STUDENTS:

1. Set up a boss and clamp stand. Attach the spring to the boss so that it can be pulled down freely. Attach a weight holder to the spring.
2. Measure the length of the spring. Record this in your results table.
3. Add one weight to the weight holder. Measure the length of the spring again. Take care to always measure between the same two points. Record this in your results table.
4. Keep adding weights to the weight holder. Record the length of the spring each time you add a weight.
5. When you have added all the weights: remove the weight holder. Measure the length of the spring again.

DATA COLLECTION IDEAS:

Weight added (N)	Length of spring (cm)

DIFFERENTIATION:

- **Decrease the challenge:** Using springs that exhibit a greater degree of stretch will make measuring the length of the spring easier.
- **Increase the challenge:** The students could repeat the investigation using elastic bands to see if they follow Hooke's law. (Care will be needed to make sure the elastic bands do not snap. Eye protection should also be worn.)

USEFUL QUESTIONS TO ASK THE STUDENTS:

1. What happened to the spring when you added the weights? Did you notice any pattern in your results?
2. What happened to the spring when you removed the weights? Why do you think this happened?
3. What do you think would have happened if we carried on adding weights to the spring? Why do you think this?

HOMEWORK:

The students can draw a graph of their results.

EXPERIMENT 76

Pattern seeking: How can we make a magnet stronger?

LEARNING OBJECTIVES:
Investigate how the number of coils on an electromagnet affects the strength of the electromagnet.

INTRODUCTION:
The students make a simple electromagnet and then test the effect of altering the number of coils on the electromagnet.

USEFUL PRIOR WORK:
The students should know what magnets are and how they work.

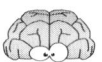

BACKGROUND SCIENCE:
A magnet is a ferrous (contains iron) material that exhibits the property of magnetism – the ability to attract iron objects. Some magnets are naturally occurring, for example lodestone. It is also possible to make a magnet by using electricity – the resulting magnet is called an electromagnet. The principle behind an electromagnet is that when a current is flowing through the magnet a magnetic field will be generated around the magnet. An electromagnet is an example of a temporary magnet as its magnetism can be switched on or off. A simple electromagnet can be built by wrapping electrical wire around an iron nail and connecting the wires to an electrical power source. The strength of an electromagnet can be increased by adding an iron core (in the case of a simple electromagnet this is the role of the iron nail), increasing the current flowing through the electromagnet or by increasing the number of coils in the electromagnet.

NATIONAL CURRICULUM LINKS:

Forces
- non-contact forces: gravity forces acting at a distance on Earth and in space, forces between magnets and forces due to static electricity.

MATERIALS NEEDED:
Large iron nails, insulated wire, power pack, crocodile clips, connecting wires, paperclips.

SAFETY AND TECHNICAL NOTES:
- The coils around the nail should not sit on top of each other as this can make the electromagnet less effective.
- The iron nail can become hot while the electromagnet is in use.
- The electromagnet should be switched off when not in use.

METHOD:

To be done in advance by the teacher

Ensure that the insulated wire the students will be using has approximately 3cm of wire exposed at each end.

STUDENTS:

1. Wrap the insulated wire around the iron nail as many times as you can. Make sure the coils are pressed up against each other but are not sitting on top of each other.
2. Attach the exposed ends of the insulated wire to the power pack using crocodile clips and connecting wires.
3. Turn on the power pack and then hold a paperclip up to the iron nail to see if it is attracted. Keep adding paperclips onto the iron nail until you are unable to add any more. Count how many paperclips you were able to add. Record this in your results table.
4. Repeat the investigation by wrapping the insulated wire around the iron nail different numbers of times. Remember to switch off your electromagnet whenever you are not using it.

DATA COLLECTION IDEAS:

No. of coils	No. of paperclips picked up

DIFFERENTIATION:
- **Decrease the challenge:** The students could work in small groups, with each group investigating a set number of coils. The results can then be pooled at the end of the investigation.
- **Increase the challenge:** The students could also investigate the effect of increasing the electric current flowing through the electromagnet.

USEFUL QUESTIONS TO ASK THE STUDENTS:

1. What happened to the strength of the electromagnet as the number of coils increased? Why do you think this happened?
2. Do you think there are any other ways to increase the strength of an electromagnet?
3. Where in everyday life do we find electromagnets?

HOMEWORK:

The students can research the Maglev train in China.

EXPERIMENT 77

Pattern seeking: How does light enter and leave a mirror?

LEARNING OBJECTIVES:
Investigate how light reflects off a mirror.

INTRODUCTION:
The students reflect light off a mirror and measure the angle of incidence and the angle of reflection.

USEFUL PRIOR WORK:
The students should know that light travels as rays.

BACKGROUND SCIENCE:
A plane mirror is the name given to any flat mirror. When light hits a mirror, it bounces off the surface of the mirror with very little scattering (this is because the surface is so smooth). This means if one distinct ray hits a mirror then one distinct ray will be reflected off the mirror. The ray of light that hits the mirror is called the incident ray. The ray of light that bounces off the mirror is called the reflected ray. The angle at which light hits a mirror is called the angle of incidence. The angle at which the light is reflected off a mirror is called the angle of reflection. The angle at which the incident ray hits the mirror is always equal to the angle the reflected ray leaves the mirror, so if light hits the mirror at an angle of 60° it will be reflected off the mirror at 60°.

NATIONAL CURRICULUM LINKS:

Light waves
- the similarities and differences between light waves and waves in matter
- light waves travelling through a vacuum; speed of light
- the transmission of light through materials: absorption, diffuse scattering and specular reflection at a surface
- use of ray model to explain imaging in mirrors, the pinhole camera, the refraction of light and action of convex lens in focusing (qualitative); the human eye.

MATERIALS NEEDED:
Ray boxes with single slit, plane mirrors, mirror holders, protractors, white card.

SAFETY AND TECHNICAL NOTES:
- The ray box will become hot with prolonged use.
- The rays of light may be difficult to see, so performing this investigation in a slightly darkened room may help the students.

METHOD:

To be done in advance by the teacher
Reduce the amount of light in the room by drawing blinds and turning off unnecessary lights.

STUDENTS:

1 Put a plane mirror into a mirror holder. Place the mirror holder onto a piece of white card.
2 Set up a ray box so that it will shine a ray of light onto the mirror. Aim a ray of light at the mirror. You should be able to see a ray of light hitting the mirror and a ray of light being reflected off the mirror.
3 Measure the angle that the ray of light is hitting the mirror. Record this in your results table.
4 Measure the angle that the ray of light is leaving the mirror. Record this in your results table.
5 Repeat the investigation by moving your ray box so that the ray of light hits the mirror at different angles.

DATA COLLECTION IDEAS:

Angle of incidence	Angle of reflection

DIFFERENTIATION:

- **Decrease the challenge:** The students may find it easier to perform this investigation on a large printout of a protractor.
- **Increase the challenge:** The students could also use additional mirrors and try to reflect the light back to the original mirror.

USEFUL QUESTIONS TO ASK THE STUDENTS:

1 What did you notice about the angle of incidence and the angle of reflection?
2 Why do you think mirrors are able to produce mirror images of objects?
3 Where in everyday life do we make use of mirrors?

HOMEWORK:

The students can research periscopes and draw how a ray of light passes through one.

EXPERIMENT 78

Pattern seeking: How can we change the speed of light?

LEARNING OBJECTIVES:
Investigate how light passes through different materials.

INTRODUCTION:
The students pass light through a Perspex block and measure the angles of incidence and refraction.

USEFUL PRIOR WORK:
The students should know that light travels as rays.

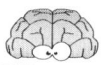

BACKGROUND SCIENCE:
When a ray of light passes from one material to another it changes speed. This is due to the density of the material the light is travelling through. The name given to this change in speed is refraction. Refraction occurs at the boundary between the different materials. The ray of light that enters the different material mirror is called the incident ray. The ray of light that passes through the different material is called the refracted ray. If the ray of light decreases in speed then the ray will bend towards the normal (an imaginary line drawn at 90° to the ray of light). If the ray of light increases in speed then the ray will bend away from the normal. The angle between the incident ray and the normal is called the angle of incidence. The angle between the refracted ray and the normal is called the angle of refraction. If a wide range of measurements are taken then the result will form a curve when plotted on a graph.

NATIONAL CURRICULUM LINKS:

Light waves
- the transmission of light through materials: absorption, diffuse scattering and specular reflection at a surface
- use of ray model to explain imaging in mirrors, the pinhole camera, the refraction of light and action of convex lens in focusing (qualitative); the human eye.

MATERIALS NEEDED:
Ray boxes with single slits, semicircular Perspex blocks, protractors, white card.

SAFETY AND TECHNICAL NOTES:
- The ray box will become hot with prolonged use.
- The bottom of the Perspex box should be painted white so the light ray can be seen passing through the block.
- The rays of light may be difficult to see, so performing this investigation in a slightly darkened room may help the students.

160 *How can we change the speed of light?*

METHOD:

To be done in advance by the teacher
Reduce the amount of light in the room by drawing blinds and turning off unnecessary lights.

STUDENTS:

1 Set up a ray box and a Perspex block onto a piece of white card. Aim a ray of light at the Perspex block so that it will travel through the block.
2 Measure the angle that the ray of light is entering the block. Record this in your results table.
3 Measure the angle that the ray of light is leaving the block. Record this in your results table.
4 Repeat the investigation by moving your ray box so that the ray of light hits the block at different angles.

DATA COLLECTION IDEAS:

Angle of incidence	Angle of refraction

DIFFERENTIATION:

- **Decrease the challenge:** The students may find it easier to perform this investigation on a large printout of a protractor.
- **Increase the challenge:** The students could draw the right-angled triangles produced and use this to calculate the sines of the angle of incidence and the angle of refraction. These results will produce a straight-line graph and will demonstrate Snell's law.

USEFUL QUESTIONS TO ASK THE STUDENTS:

1 What happened to the ray of light as it passed from the air into the Perspex block and from the Perspex block into the air? Why do you think this happened?
2 What did you notice about the angle of incidence and the angle of refraction?
3 Where in everyday life do we make use of refraction?

HOMEWORK:

The students can research how optical fibres make use of total internal reflection.

EXPERIMENT 79

Pattern seeking: What happens to waves in shallow water?

LEARNING OBJECTIVES:
Investigate how waves pass through water of different depths.

INTRODUCTION:
The students observe waves in a ripple tank in order to see how they are refracted as the depth of the water in the tank changes.

USEFUL PRIOR WORK:
The students should know the names of the different parts of a wave.

BACKGROUND SCIENCE:
Waves that travel through water can be refracted in a similar way to light waves. Waves travel faster in deep water than they do in shallow water (this is due to the drag effect produced by the friction of the waves passing over the ground). If waves change speed due to a change in the depth of the water then their direction will also change. This is similar to when light is refracted as it passes from one medium to another medium – the speed of the light will change causing it to change direction. The refracted waves passing through the shallow water will have a shorter wavelength than the waves passing through the deeper water. These effects can be observed by setting up a ripple tank with a glass plate. The glass plate will make the water shallower and the waves will be refracted around the glass plate.

NATIONAL CURRICULUM LINKS:

Observed waves
- waves on water as undulations which travel through water with transverse motion; these waves can be reflected, and add or cancel – superposition.

MATERIALS NEEDED:
Ripple tank and accessories, motor, glass plate, overhead projector (optional).

SAFETY AND TECHNICAL NOTES:
- This investigation is best performed as a demonstration.
- Placing the ripple tank onto an overhead projector will allow the waves to be projected onto the screen, allowing them to be seen more easily.

METHOD:

To be done in advance by the teacher
Set up the ripple tank and motor.

162   What happens to waves in shallow water?

STUDENTS:

1 Set up a ripple tank and overhead projector if you are using one.
2 Place the glass plate into the ripple tank so that it is parallel to the vibrating beam.
3 Have the students observe the waves and how they pass the glass plate.
4 Place the glass plate at different angles and have the students observe the change in direction of the waves.

DATA COLLECTION IDEAS:

The students can draw diagrams of what they observe.

DIFFERENTIATION:

- **Decrease the challenge:** Projecting the waves onto a screen and using a ruler may help the students notice the changes to the waves.
- **Increase the challenge:** The students can observe waves with different frequencies to see what happens when they are refracted.

USEFUL QUESTIONS TO ASK THE STUDENTS:

1 What did you observe about the waves and how they travelled through the water? Why do you think this happened?
2 Was there any pattern in how the waves changed direction as the depth of the water changed?
3 Are there any similarities or differences between how these waves behaved and how light behaves when it is refracted?

HOMEWORK:

The students can investigate how lenses work (concave and convex) and how waves pass through them.

EXPERIMENT 80

Classification and identification: Which materials are best for keeping something warm?

LEARNING OBJECTIVES:
Classify a selection of materials as either thermal conductors or thermal insulators.

INTRODUCTION:
The students test some common household objects in order to classify them as either thermal conductors or thermal insulators based on how well they maintain the temperature of a beaker of hot water.

USEFUL PRIOR WORK:
The students should understand the terms conductor and insulator.

BACKGROUND SCIENCE:
Heat is a type of energy. Like other types of energy, heat can be transferred from one place to another. The modes by which heat can be transferred are conduction, convection and radiation. Conduction of heat occurs via the particles that make up a substance. The energy from the heat causes the particles that make up the substance to vibrate with more energy. This causes heat to be conducted from the hot end of the substance to the cold end. Metals are examples of good conductors of heat. Non-metals do not generally conduct heat well and are referred to as insulators. Convection of heat occurs in liquids and gases. Convection currents form that cause hot particles to rise and cold particles fall to take their place. These convection currents help to spread the heat energy throughout the liquid or gas. Infrared (thermal) radiation is a type of electromagnetic radiation. This means that the heat energy travels via waves rather than via particles. All objects give off some level of infrared radiation.

NATIONAL CURRICULUM LINKS:

Energy changes and transfers
- heating and thermal equilibrium: temperature difference between two objects leading to energy transfer from the hotter to the cooler one, through contact (conduction) or radiation; such transfers tending to reduce the temperature difference; use of insulators.

MATERIALS NEEDED:
Large beakers, small beakers with cardboard lids, thermometers, kettle, timers, a selection of materials to test (for example, cotton wool, newspaper, cling film, tin foil, greaseproof paper, cotton fabric).

SAFETY AND TECHNICAL NOTES:
- The students should take care when using boiling water.

METHOD:

To be done in advance by the teacher
Make sure all the materials that will be tested are approximately the same size.

Best materials for keeping something warm

STUDENTS:

1. Add 100ml of boiling water to a beaker. Place the lid onto the beaker and place a thermometer in the beaker through the hole in the lid.
2. Take the temperature of the water. Record this in your results table.
3. Take the temperature of the water every minute for 5 minutes. Record the results in your results table.
4. Repeat steps 1–3 but wrap the beaker in a different material each time.

DATA COLLECTION IDEAS:

Material	Temp. of water (°C) at					
	0 min	1 min	2 mins	3 mins	4 mins	5 mins

DIFFERENTIATION:
- **Decrease the challenge:** The students can work in small groups with each group investigating one material. The results can then be pooled at the end of the investigation.
- **Increase the challenge:** The students can use the results to plan a fair-test style investigation into thermal conduction and insulation.

USEFUL QUESTIONS TO ASK THE STUDENTS:
1. Which materials were the best and worst at insulating the beaker? Why do you think this was?
2. How was heat energy able to leave the water in the beaker?
3. What do you think happened to the heat energy that escaped from the beaker?

HOMEWORK:
The students can research infrared cameras including how they work and their uses.

EXPERIMENT 81

Classification and identification: Which materials are best for building an electric circuit?

LEARNING OBJECTIVES:
Classify a selection of materials as either electrical conductors or electrical insulators.

INTRODUCTION:
The students build a simple electrical circuit and use it to test some common household objects in order to classify them as either electrical conductors or electrical insulators.

USEFUL PRIOR WORK:
The students should know how to build a simple electrical circuit.

BACKGROUND SCIENCE:
An electrical circuit allows electricity to flow through it and power an electrical device. In order to do this the circuit must be both complete and composed from materials that are conductors. Conductors are materials that allow electricity to easily flow through them. Insulators, on the other hand, are materials that do not allow electricity to flow through them. Metals are conductors of electricity, although how well they conduct electricity varies between the different metals. Gold and copper are examples of metals that have high conductivity values. Metals are able to conduct electricity due to the presence of free electrons in the outer shell of metal atoms. These electrons are able to carry the electrical current. There are some non-metals that are able to conduct electricity; these include graphite and salt water.

NATIONAL CURRICULUM LINKS:

Electricity and electromagnetism
- differences in resistance between conducting and insulating components (quantitative).

MATERIALS NEEDED:
Power packs, connecting wires, crocodile clips, bulb in bulb holder, a selection of materials to test (for example, wooden ruler, paper cup, graphite pencil, two pence coin, metal spoon, rubber, elastic band, tin foil etc.).

SAFETY AND TECHNICAL NOTES:
- The bulbs can become hot after prolonged use.

METHOD:

To be done in advance by the teacher
Have a selection of materials prepared for the students to test. Make sure they are a suitable size to use in the electrical circuits.

Materials to build an electric circuit

STUDENTS:

1 Build a simple circuit using the powerpack, connecting wires, crocodile clips and bulb. Make sure the bulb lights up when the circuit is connected.
2 Make a gap in the circuit and place the first material you will be testing into the gap. Connect the material to the circuit using connecting wires.
3 Observe whether the bulb lights up. Decide if the material you tested is a conductor or an insulator.
4 Repeat the investigation for the rest of the materials.

DATA COLLECTION IDEAS:

Material	Did the bulb light up?	Conductor or insulator?

DIFFERENTIATION:
- **Decrease the challenge:** The students can have the electrical circuit premade for them so they only have to add the material they are testing.
- **Increase the challenge:** The students can test a selection of different metals and attempt to rank them in order of conductivity based on the brightness of a bulb in the circuit.

USEFUL QUESTIONS TO ASK THE STUDENTS:
1 Which materials were conductors/insulators? Did any of your results surprise you?
2 Why might we want to build some parts of an electrical circuit out of insulating materials?
3 Do you think all metals conduct electricity equally well? Why do you think this?

HOMEWORK:
The students can research superconductors including their properties and uses.

EXPERIMENT 82

Classification and identification: Can we identify different types of radiation?

LEARNING OBJECTIVES:
Identify three different types of radiation.

INTRODUCTION:
The students observe a Geiger-Müller tube and counter as it is exposed to alpha, beta and gamma radiation.

USEFUL PRIOR WORK:
The students should know that some materials emit radiation.

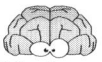

BACKGROUND SCIENCE:
Nuclear radiation is a type of energy given off from the nucleus of an atom. There are three types of nuclear radiation–alpha, beta and gamma. A material that gives off radiation is called a radioactive source. Nuclear radiation can be harmful to living organisms as it can cause mutations to occur in a cell's DNA. However, humans can be exposed to low levels of 'background radiation' (radiation that naturally exists in the environment) without any ill effect. Of the three types of nuclear radiation, alpha is the least penetrating and gamma is the most penetrating. The different types of radiation can also be stopped by different materials. Alpha radiation can be stopped by a single sheet of paper. Beta radiation can be stopped by a thin sheet of aluminium. Gamma radiation can only be stopped by a thick sheet of lead. The different types of radiation are also able to travel for different distances. Alpha radiation can travel a few centimetres, beta radiation can travel about a metre and gamma radiation can travel several metres.

NATIONAL CURRICULUM LINKS:

Energy in matter
- internal energy stored in materials.

MATERIALS NEEDED:
Combined Geiger-Müller tube and counter (available from www.mindsetsonline.co.uk), sealed alpha source, sealed beta source, sealed gamma source, holders for radioactive sources, white paper, aluminium, lead.

SAFETY AND TECHNICAL NOTES:

- This investigation must be carried out as a demonstration by the teacher.
- Do not allow the students to handle any sources of radiation.
- Only remove one radioactive source from its container at any one time.

168 *Identifying different types of radiation*

METHOD:

To be done in advance by the teacher
Set up the Geiger-Müller tube and counter. Follow all school procedures for using radioactive sources.

1 Set up a Geiger-Müller tube and counter. Take the first radioactive source and point it at the Geiger-Müller tube and counter. Have the students make notes on their observations. Repeat with the other radioactive sources.
2 Repeat the investigation but this time hold up the different materials – paper, aluminium and lead – to demonstrate how the different radiations are stopped. Have the students make notes on their observations.
3 Repeat the investigation but this time hold the radioactive sources at different distances from the Geiger-Müller tube and counter to demonstrate that the different types of radiation can travel different distances in air.

DATA COLLECTION IDEAS:
The students can make notes on their observations.

DIFFERENTIATION:
- **Decrease the challenge:** Recording the demonstration and playing it back for the students may allow them more opportunity to observe what is happening.
- **Increase the challenge:** The students can observe different sources of alpha, beta and gamma radiation to see if there are any similarities or differences between them.

USEFUL QUESTIONS TO ASK THE STUDENTS:
1 What did you observe about the three different types of radiation?
2 Why do you think the different types of radiation can be stopped by different materials?
3 Why do you think exposure to high levels of radiation is damaging to our bodies?

HOMEWORK:
The students can research the uses of the different types of radiation.

EXPERIMENT 83

Classification and identification: Can we classify all materials as solids, liquids or gases?

LEARNING OBJECTIVES:
Classify different substances as solids, liquids or gases.

INTRODUCTION:
The students examine a number of different substances and classify them as solids, liquids or gases based on their properties.

USEFUL PRIOR WORK:
The students should know the three states of matter.

BACKGROUND SCIENCE:
Three examples of states of matter are solids, liquids and gases (plasma is another example). The particle model explains the different properties that solids, liquids and gases exhibit. The particles in a solid are packed very tightly together. The particles are not able to move freely but do vibrate in their fixed positions. As a result, solids have a fixed shape, cannot flow and cannot be squashed or compressed. The particles in a liquid are held close together in a random arrangement. The particles can move around each other so can therefore flow and will take the shape of their container. Liquids have a fixed volume and cannot be squashed or compressed. The particles in a gas are far apart from each other in random arrangements. The particles are able to move freely so can therefore flow and will fill their container. As there is a large amount of space between the particles in a gas they can be compressed so therefore do not have a fixed volume.

NATIONAL CURRICULUM LINKS:

Physical changes
- similarities and differences, including density differences, between solids, liquids and gases.

Particle model
- the differences in arrangements, in motion and in closeness of particles explaining changes of state, shape and density; the anomaly of ice-water transition
- atoms and molecules as particles.

MATERIALS NEEDED:
A selection of materials for the students to examine including, ice cubes, water, custard, shampoo, lemon juice, wood blocks, flower petals, wax, greaseproof paper, table salt, chocolate chips, toothpaste, shaving foam, glass blocks, pumice stone, sponge, chalk, cardboard box, balloon filled with air, balloon filled with carbon dioxide, balloon filled with hydrogen.

SAFETY AND TECHNICAL NOTES:
- Fill any balloons just before the start of the investigation.
- Remind the students not to consume any food products.

170 *Materials: all solids, liquids or gases?*

- Be aware of any allergies.
- The students should wash their hands after the investigation.
- Eye protection may be required depending on what substances are used in the investigation.

METHOD:

To be done in advance by the teacher

Have the samples ready for the students to examine. The students can move around the room and examine the substances in small groups. You may want to include magnifying lenses and balances to aid the students' observations.

STUDENTS:

1. Examine each of the substances you have been given. Make notes on their appearance, texture, smell and properties.
2. Decide whether you would classify the substance as a solid, liquid or a gas. Record your results in your results table.

DATA COLLECTION IDEAS:

Substance	Observations	Solid, liquid or gas?

DIFFERENTIATION:

- **Decrease the challenge:** Providing prompt questions for each substance might help the students with their observations, for example, 'could you pour this substance?'.
- **Increase the challenge:** The students can observe non-Newtonian fluids and try to decide how they should be classified. Oobleck (cornflour and water) is a good example. The students can hit a bowl of Oobleck with a rubber mat and observe what happens.

USEFUL QUESTIONS TO ASK THE STUDENTS:

1. Did you manage to classify all the substances as solids, liquids or gases? Were any substances difficult to classify?
2. Why are we able to pour liquids and gases but not solids?
3. Why did the properties of the different solids you observed vary from each other?

HOMEWORK:

The students can research the state of matter of plasma including its uses.

EXPERIMENT 84

Classification and identification: What is the densest liquid?

LEARNING OBJECTIVES:
Identify the relative densities of a range of liquids by making a density column.

INTRODUCTION:
The students use a selection of different liquids to make a density column in order to identify the order of density for the liquids.

USEFUL PRIOR WORK:
The students should be familiar with the term density.

BACKGROUND SCIENCE:
The density of a liquid is the quantity of mass of a liquid in a certain volume. The calculation for density is mass divided by volume. This means that liquids with more space between the particles will have a lower density than liquids that have very tightly packed together particles. A liquid with a high density will usually appear to be very thick and/or viscous, whereas liquids with a low density will usually appear very thin and runny. Liquids with a high density will be able to exert a greater upwards force than a liquid with a lower density. This means that liquids with a low density will be able to float on top of liquids with a higher density. This can be demonstrated by making a density column where liquids with different densities are added to a tall container. The liquids will eventually settle into layers, with the liquids with higher densities nearer the bottom of the container. The unit for density is either g/cm^3 or g/mL.

NATIONAL CURRICULUM LINKS:

Physical changes
- similarities and differences, including density differences, between solids, liquids and gases.

Particle model
- the differences in arrangements, in motion and in closeness of particles explaining changes of state, shape and density; the anomaly of ice-water transition.

MATERIALS NEEDED:
Tall beakers, measuring cylinders, funnels, water, washing-up liquid, syrup, honey, cooking oil, rubbing alcohol, milk, molasses.

SAFETY AND TECHNICAL NOTES:
- Remind the students not to consume any of the liquids.
- Rubbing alcohol is flammable and an irritant to the eyes.
- Other liquids can be substituted for the ones that are listed. Make sure any choices are safe for the students to handle.
- The students should wash their hands after the investigation.

METHOD:

To be done in advance by the teacher
Have the different liquids set out in large, labelled beakers.

STUDENTS:

1. Set up a tall beaker and a funnel. Select the first liquid you will be adding to your column. Measure out 25ml of the liquid using a measuring cylinder.
2. Very carefully pour the liquid into the beaker. Use the funnel to make sure the liquid falls into the centre of the beaker and does not coat the sides of the beaker.
3. Choose the next liquid you will be adding to the column. Add this liquid to your column in the same way. Allow the liquids some time to settle before you add the next liquid.
4. Add the rest of the liquids in the same way. Leave some time between each liquid to allow them to settle.
5. When you have added all the liquids and they have settled into distinct layers, draw your density column and write out the names of the liquids in order of density.

DATA COLLECTION IDEAS:
The students can draw their resulting density columns.

DIFFERENTIATION:
- **Decrease the challenge:** The students may need help pouring the liquids into the beaker.
- **Increase the challenge:** The students could also add small objects to their density columns, for example a penny, to see which layer they settle in.

USEFUL QUESTIONS TO ASK THE STUDENTS:
1. Which of the liquids has the greatest and lowest density? How do you know this?
2. Why do liquids have different densities?
3. How might this information be useful to us in everyday life?

HOMEWORK:
The students can research oil spills including their impact and how they can be cleaned up.

EXPERIMENT 85

Classification and identification: Where is the energy going?

LEARNING OBJECTIVES:
Identify the energy transfers taking place in household objects.

INTRODUCTION:
The students observe a selection of household objects and identify any energy transfers taking place.

USEFUL PRIOR WORK:
The students should know that energy can be transferred from one type of energy to another.

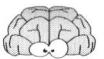

BACKGROUND SCIENCE:
The law of the conservation of energy states that energy cannot be created nor destroyed, only transferred from one type of energy to another. An electrical lamp, for example, converts electrical energy to light and heat. The light that is produced is an example of useful energy (energy that we want to be produced). The heat that is produced is an example of wasted energy (energy that we do not want to be produced). The energy transfers taking place can be represented by Sankey diagrams that show the relative amounts of the different types of energy being produced. It is also possible to calculate the efficiency of a device by dividing the amount of useful energy produced by the total amount of energy going into the device.

NATIONAL CURRICULUM LINKS:

Energy changes and transfers
- other processes that involve energy transfer: changing motion, dropping an object, completing an electrical circuit, stretching a spring, metabolism of food, burning fuels.

MATERIALS NEEDED:
A selection of objects to demonstrate energy transfers – good examples include a kettle, a hairdryer, a lamp, a toaster, a radio, a skipping rope, a ball, a remote control car, a wind-up toy, electrical circuit with a motor, loudspeaker.

SAFETY AND TECHNICAL NOTES:
- Supervise students when they are using electrical devices.

METHOD:

To be done in advance by the teacher
Set up the electrical devices the students will be using. Test them to make sure they will work.

174 *Where is the energy going?*

STUDENTS:

Examine the items you have been given. For each one observe and determine:

1. Where is the energy coming from?
2. What type of energy/s is it being transferred to?
3. Which of these energies are useful?
4. Which ones are examples of wasted energy?
5. Record your observations.

DATA COLLECTION IDEAS:
The students can make notes on their observations.

DIFFERENTIATION:
- **Decrease the challenge:** The students can be given cards with different examples of energy transfers on them to help them identify the energy transfers taking place.
- **Increase the challenge:** The students can draw energy transfer diagrams for the items in the investigation.

USEFUL QUESTIONS TO ASK THE STUDENTS:
1. Which energy transfers did you observe? Were all the energy transfers you observed useful energy transfers?
2. How could we reduce the amounts of wasted energy produced by some devices?
3. What energy transfers take place in our bodies when we eat food?

HOMEWORK:
The students can research different types of renewable energy and how they work.

EXPERIMENT 86

Modelling:
Can we cook food using the sun?

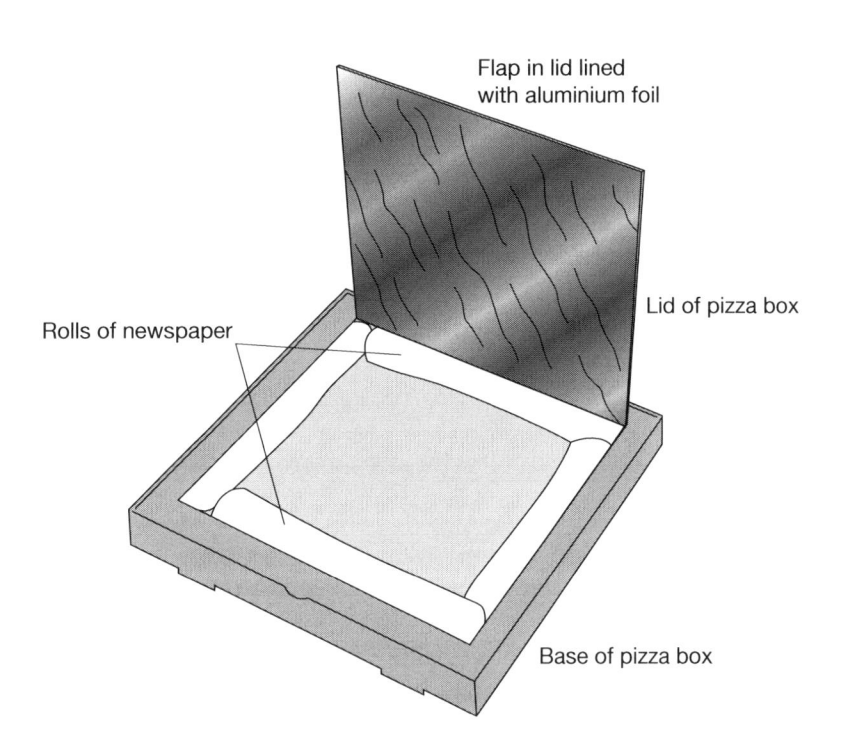

Flap in lid lined with aluminium foil

Rolls of newspaper

Lid of pizza box

Base of pizza box

LEARNING OBJECTIVES:
Make a solar-powered oven.

INTRODUCTION:
The students design and make a model solar-powered oven and use it to cook.

USEFUL PRIOR WORK:
The students should know about solar-powered energy.

BACKGROUND SCIENCE:
A solar oven is a basic oven that uses only the heat from the sun in order to cook food. It is constructed from a cardboard box lined with aluminium foil and black paper. The aluminium foil reflects the heat from the sun into the box and the black paper lining the oven absorbs the heat. These types of solar ovens are called 'collector boxes' as they work on the principle of collecting the energy (in the form of heat) from the sun and using it to cook the food that is inside the box. Solar ovens work better on hot days with the oven placed in direct sunlight. Solar ovens can reach temperatures of 200ºF on hot days. However, as solar ovens are only using solar power they will take longer to cook food than a conventional oven. Due to the fact that the temperature cannot be controlled or measured precisely, it is better to use solar ovens to cook 'low risk' foods, for example making cheese on toast.

NATIONAL CURRICULUM LINKS:

Energy
- fuels and energy resources

176 *Can we cook food using the sun?*

- heating and thermal equilibrium: temperature difference between two objects leading to energy transfer from the hotter to the cooler one, through contact (conduction) or radiation; such transfers tending to reduce the temperature difference: use of insulators.

MATERIALS NEEDED:
Shallow, square cardboard boxes (for example, the boxes that pizzas come in), aluminium foil, black sugar paper, sellotape, cling film, newspaper, rulers, scissors or craft knives, rulers.

SAFETY AND TECHNICAL NOTES:
- This investigation is best done in the summer during warm, sunny weather.
- Use the solar oven to cook low risk foods, for example melting cheese or heating beans.
- You may want to build an oven in advance so that the students have an idea of how it is constructed.
- As the solar ovens take a long time to cook food you may want to build the ovens one day and then test them on another day.
- Check for any allergies.

METHOD:

To be done in advance by the teacher
Have a suitable spot and foods prepared to test the solar ovens.

STUDENTS:

1. Open the box that you will be using to make your solar-powered oven. Cover the bottom of the box with black sugar paper. Use sellotape to hold the paper in place.
2. Roll up a sheet of newspaper into a tube and line one edge inside the box. Hold it in place with sellotape. Do this for the remaining three sides.
3. Cut a flap into the lid of the cardboard box. Use a ruler to measure a square that leaves a border approximately 2cm wide in the cardboard box. Cut the three edges of the square leaving one edge uncut to act as a hinge.
4. Line the inside of the flap you just made with aluminium foil. Use sellotape to hold it in place.
5. Cover the hole you just made in the lid using cling film. Use sellotape to hold it in place.
6. Line the entire inside of the box with aluminium foil (cover the black paper and newspaper).
7. When you use the oven: lift up the lid of the box and place the food you will be cooking inside. Close the lid and lift up the flap. Use a ruler to keep the flap up. The flap should be proximally 45° so that it reflects heat back into the oven.

DATA COLLECTION IDEAS:
The students can take photographs of their solar ovens and what they have cooked in them and write instructions for how to build a solar oven.

DIFFERENTIATION:
- **Decrease the challenge:** The students can be given assistance with building the solar ovens.
- **Increase the challenge:** The students could conduct a fair-test style investigation using their solar ovens in order to see which food cooks best in the oven.

USEFUL QUESTIONS TO ASK THE STUDENTS:
1. Why were our solar ovens able to cook the food inside them?
2. Why did we line our solar ovens with black paper and aluminium foil?
3. What are the advantages and disadvantages of using solar ovens for cooking food?

HOMEWORK:
The students could research other uses of solar power.

EXPERIMENT 87

Modelling:
Can we make our own camera?

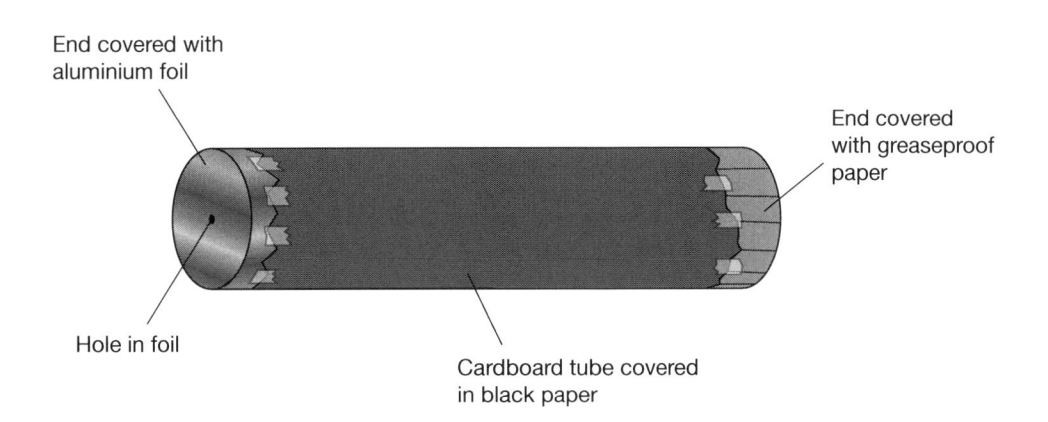

Diagram labels: End covered with aluminium foil; Hole in foil; Cardboard tube covered in black paper; End covered with greaseproof paper

LEARNING OBJECTIVES:
Design and make a pinhole camera.

INTRODUCTION:
The students use a cardboard tube to construct a basic pinhole camera.

USEFUL PRIOR WORK:
The students should know how light travels.

BACKGROUND SCIENCE:
A pinhole camera is an example of a *camera obscura*, which means 'dark chamber'. These camera obscuras were originally dark rooms where light entered through a small hole in one wall, projecting the image outside the room onto the opposite wall in the room. A pinhole camera works in a similar way. A pinhole camera consists of a light-proof box, a small hole and something to act as the photographic film, usually a semi-transparent paper. Light enters through the pinhole in the camera and is focused onto the paper at the back of the pinhole camera. The image produced by the pinhole camera will be upside down and smaller than the real life image. Traditional film-based cameras work in the same way as pinhole cameras but they are able to produce a better image and the image is projected onto photographic film that will produce a permanent image.

NATIONAL CURRICULUM LINKS:

Light waves
- the transmission of light through materials: absorption, diffuse scattering and specular reflection at a surface
- use of ray model to explain imaging in mirrors, the pinhole camera, the refraction of light and action of convex lens in focusing (qualitative); the human eye.

MATERIALS NEEDED:
Empty cardboard tubes (for example, toilet roll tube), aluminium foil, greaseproof paper, scissors, sellotape, black sugar paper, pins, lightbox or torch.

⚠ SAFETY AND TECHNICAL NOTES:

- Performing this investigation in a slightly darkened room may help the students see the images in their pinhole camera.

METHOD:

To be done in advance by the teacher
Reduce the amount of light in the room by drawing blinds and turning off unnecessary lights. Make sure the room is still light enough for the students to move around safely.

STUDENTS:

1. Take an empty cardboard tube and cover one end with aluminium foil. Make sure there are no gaps. Hold the aluminium foil in place securely with sellotape.
2. Cover the other end of the tube with greaseproof paper. Make sure there are no gaps. Hold the greaseproof paper in place securely with sellotape.
3. Cover the length of the tube in black sugar paper. Make sure the sugar paper does not cover the ends of the tube. Hold the sugar paper in place securely with sellotape.
4. Use the pin to make a small hole in the middle of the aluminium foil.
5. Hold the cardboard tube up to the lightbox or torch. The aluminium foil end should be closest to the lightbox or torch.
6. Look at the greaseproof paper. Move the tube until you can see a clear image on the greaseproof paper. Record what you observe.
7. Use the pin to make the hole in the aluminium foil slightly bigger. Hold the tube up to the light again and record what you observe.
8. Use the pin to make the hole in the aluminium foil slightly bigger one more time. Hold the tube up to the light again and record what you observe.

✎ DATA COLLECTION IDEAS:

The students can draw an annotated diagram of their pinhole camera including the rays of light passing through the camera and what they observed.

DIFFERENTIATION:

- **Decrease the challenge:** The students can be assisted with making the pinhole camera.
- **Increase the challenge:** The students can observe what happens when they increase the number of pinholes in the camera.

USEFUL QUESTIONS TO ASK THE STUDENTS:

1. What did you observe when you held your camera up to the light? Why did this happen?
2. What happened as you increased the size of the hole? Why do you think this happened?
3. In what ways is the pinhole camera we made similar to our eyes?

HOMEWORK:

The students can research the history and development of cameras.

EXPERIMENT 88

Modelling:
How can a potato be a battery?

LEARNING OBJECTIVES:
Power an electric circuit using just a potato.

INTRODUCTION:
The students build a simple electric circuit and use a potato as the 'battery'.

USEFUL PRIOR WORK:
The students should know how to build a simple circuit and the role of a battery.

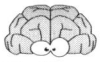

BACKGROUND SCIENCE:
Ordinary batteries produce an electrical current due to a chemical reaction taking place inside the battery. They therefore act as energy stores and can be used to power an electric circuit. A battery contains an electrolyte (a solution that will conduct electricity), typically an acidic solution, and has an electrode at each end, which act as a positive and a negative electrode. A potato can be used as a battery in an electric circuit. Potatoes contain a weak acid (phosphoric acid) that can act as an electrolyte. Small strips of metal can be added to the potato to act as the electrodes. The electricity will flow through the potato in the same way as a normal battery. The potato battery will not be very strong however, so would only be able to power a circuit that did not require much power.

NATIONAL CURRICULUM LINKS:

Electricity and electromagnetism
- electric current, measured in amperes, in circuits, series and parallel circuits, currents add where branches meet and current as flow of charge
- potential difference, measured in volts, battery and bulb ratings; resistance, measured in ohms, as the ratio of potential difference (p.d.) to current
- differences in resistance between conducting and insulating components (quantitative).

MATERIALS NEEDED:
Potatoes, metal strips to act as electrodes (copper, zinc and magnesium), crocodile clips, connecting wires, voltmeter, LEDs.

SAFETY AND TECHNICAL NOTES:
- Keep the magnesium strips away from any heat source.

METHOD:

To be done in advance by the teacher
The potatoes can be cut in half to reduce the number needed for the investigation.

STUDENTS:

1. Take a potato and push one copper strip and one zinc strip into the potato. The metal strips should not touch each other and should not come out the other side of the potato.
2. Attach a connecting wire to each metal strip using a crocodile clip. Attach the other ends of the connecting wires to the voltmeter. Record the reading on the voltmeter.
3. Replace the voltmeter with an LED. Record whether the LED lights up.
4. Repeat the investigation using a copper strip and a magnesium strip.
5. Repeat the investigation with a magnesium strip and a zinc strip.

DATA COLLECTION IDEAS:
The students can draw annotated diagrams of their final battery.

DIFFERENTIATION:
- **Decrease the challenge:** The students can be assisted with constructing the circuit.
- **Increase the challenge:** The students could also test different fruits and vegetables to see if they achieve the same results.

USEFUL QUESTIONS TO ASK THE STUDENTS:

1. What factors affected how well the battery worked? Why do you think this happened?
2. What do you think would happen if we connected lots of potatoes together and used them as a battery? Why do you think this?
3. Could vegetable batteries be used to help solve the world's energy crisis? Why do you think this?

HOMEWORK:
The students could produce an illustrated guide on how to build and use a potato battery.

EXPERIMENT 89

Modelling:
Can we build a catapult?

LEARNING OBJECTIVES:
Make a model catapult and test how well it launches a cotton wool ball.

INTRODUCTION:
The students build a model catapult and test how well it launches a cotton wool ball towards a target.

USEFUL PRIOR WORK:
The students should be familiar with forces and gravity.

BACKGROUND SCIENCE:
Catapults are medieval inventions that were typically used in battle situations, particularly for launching projectiles over castle walls. A projectile's motion is controlled by two different forces. The first force is gravity, which pulls the object towards the ground. The second force is the one causing the object to move forwards. The scientist Galileo proved that the path a projectile takes up into the air is a mirror image of the path it takes back down to the ground. This means that if the projectile is launched from a steeper angle then it will go higher into the air but will not travel as far before it comes back down to the ground. The path a projectile takes can be plotted on a graph and it will form a curve that is called a parabola. The optimum launch angle for a projectile is 45°.

NATIONAL CURRICULUM LINKS:

Forces
- forces as pushes or pulls, arising from the interaction between two objects
- using force arrows in diagrams, adding forces in one dimension, balanced and unbalanced forces
- forces: associated with deforming objects; stretching and squashing – springs; with rubbing and friction between surfaces, with pushing things out of the way; resistance to motion of air and water
- forces being needed to cause objects to stop or start moving, or to change their speed or direction of motion (qualitative only)
- change depending on direction of force and its size.

MATERIALS NEEDED:
Wooden sticks (for example, lolly pop sticks), rubber bands, small metal tray, cotton wool, glue, paper plates, timers (optional).

SAFETY AND TECHNICAL NOTES:
- Using cotton wool balls for this investigation reduces the risk of injury from flying projectiles.

METHOD:

To be done in advance by the teacher
Have a suitable space for the students to test their catapults.

STUDENTS:

1. Place six wooden sticks on top of each other. Hold them together at each end with elastic bands. Make sure they are held securely together.
2. Place one wooden stick on top of the stack in the middle so that it forms a cross. Hold this stick in place with glue. When the glue has dried, turn the sticks over so that the single stick is touching the table.
3. Glue a foil tray to the end of another wooden stick. When the glue has dried, use an elastic band to attach this wooden stick to one end of the single stick. Make sure it is held securely in place.
4. Test your catapult to make sure it works. Place a cotton wool ball into the foil tray. Press the lolly stick with the foil tray down as far as it will go and then release the stick.
5. Make a target to test your catapult. Use a paper plate and draw a cross in the centre.
6. Test your catapult and see what happens when you alter how far down you press the lolly stick and how far away you have the catapult from the target. How many times can you hit the cross on your target?

DATA COLLECTION IDEAS:

The students can take photographs of their finished catapults and write instructions for how to build one.

DIFFERENTIATION:

- **Decrease the challenge:** The students can make a simple catapult from a rubber band threaded through two holes in a lolly stick.
- **Increase the challenge:** The students can attempt to measure the angle they are launching their cotton wool from by using a protractor.

USEFUL QUESTIONS TO ASK THE STUDENTS:

1. What happened when you altered how far down you pushed the launching stick? Why do you think this happened?
2. What happened when you altered how far away you placed your catapult from the target? Why do you think this happened?
3. What other factors might affect how the catapult launches the cotton wool?

HOMEWORK:

The students can draw force diagrams for the catapult before, during and after launching the cotton wool.

EXPERIMENT 90

Modelling:
Can we design and make a musical instrument?

LEARNING OBJECTIVES:
Design and build a musical instrument.

INTRODUCTION:
The students use a selection of materials to design and build a musical instrument capable of producing a range of different 'notes'.

USEFUL PRIOR WORK:
The students should know how sounds are made.

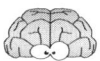

BACKGROUND SCIENCE:
Sounds are produced when an object vibrates and those vibrations pass through the air and into our ears (this is why sound cannot travel in a vacuum as it needs a medium to travel through). Pitch is one particular property of sound. It is caused by the frequency that the object is vibrating – higher frequencies of vibrations result in a higher pitched sound, whilst lower frequencies of vibrations result in a lower pitched sound. The frequency of a sound is measured in hertz (Hz). In terms of musical instruments, it is typically the size of the vibrating part of the instrument that causes the frequency of vibrations and therefore the pitched produced. For string instruments, a shorter string will typically produce a higher pitch, for percussion instruments (note that there are not many tuneable percussion instruments) a tighter 'skin' on a drum will produce a higher pitch, and for wind instruments a shorter column of air will produce a higher pitch.

NATIONAL CURRICULUM LINKS:

Waves
- frequencies of sound waves, measured in hertz (Hz); echoes, reflection and absorption of sound
- sound needs a medium to travel, the speed of sound in air, in water, in solids.

MATERIALS NEEDED:
Selection of materials for building a musical instrument, for example, drinking straws of different diameters, nylon string, elastic bands, metal wire, cardboard boxes of different sizes, cardboard tubes of different diameters, balloons, glass bottles, boiling tubes etc., scissors, sellotape, glue.

SAFETY AND TECHNICAL NOTES:
- String or wire that is pulled very tight may snap and cause eye damage. Eye protection could be worn by students using these materials.

METHOD:

To be done in advance by the teacher
Prepare a selection of materials for the students to use for their instruments.

STUDENTS:

1. Examine the materials you have been given to make your musical instrument. Decide in your group what type of instrument you want to make.
2. Sketch a rough design of your instrument and identify what materials you will use and how you will get your instrument to produce different notes.
3. Choose your materials and build your instrument. When it is complete, test your instrument and see how many different notes it is able to produce. Can you improve it in any way so that it will make more notes?
4. Play your instrument for the rest of the class!

DATA COLLECTION IDEAS:

The students can draw and label their musical instruments and identify how the different notes are produced. A recording could be made of the musical instruments produced by the class.

DIFFERENTIATION:

- **Decrease the challenge:** The students can be given the materials required to make a particular type of musical instrument, for example pan-pipes, and challenged to design and build the instrument.
- **Increase the challenge:** The students can be challenged to build an instrument that can be played in more than one way, for example water bottles that can be struck with a drumstick or blown across the top, and investigate how the pitch changes for each method.

USEFUL QUESTIONS TO ASK THE STUDENTS:

1. What is vibrating in your musical instrument in order to produce the sound?
2. How are you able to change the pitch of the sound produced?
3. Is there any way we could tune our instruments so that we know which musical note is being produced when we play them?

HOMEWORK:

The students can research a particular musical instrument including its origins, how it is played and how different sounds are produced.

EXPERIMENT 91

Modelling:
Can we make a crash helmet?

LEARNING OBJECTIVES:
Design and build a crash helmet.

INTRODUCTION:
The students build a model crash helmet that will be used to protect an egg when dropped from a one-metre height.

USEFUL PRIOR WORK:
The students should know what a force is and that different materials have different properties.

BACKGROUND SCIENCE:
A force is something that can change the shape, speed, or direction of an object. Gravity is an example of a force, as unsupported objects will fall towards the Earth because of the effects of gravity. As an object falls it accelerates (increases its speed) up to its maximum terminal velocity. When a falling object comes into contact with the ground it stops suddenly. This contact force from the ground can cause damage to the object. In order to protect a falling object this contact force from the ground needs to be minimised. This can be achieved by slowing down the rate at which the object falls, for example with parachute style devices, or by using another material to absorb some of the contact force from the ground, for example by using devices that make use of padding.

NATIONAL CURRICULUM LINKS:

Forces
- forces as pushes or pulls, arising from the interaction between two objects
- using force arrows in diagrams, adding forces in one dimension, balanced and unbalanced forces
- forces: associated with deforming objects; stretching and squashing – springs; with rubbing and friction between surfaces, with pushing things out of the way; resistance to motion of air and water
- forces measured in newtons, measurements of stretch or compression as force is changed
- non-contact forces: gravity forces acting at a distance on Earth and in space, forces between magnets, and forces due to static electricity.

MATERIALS NEEDED:
Eggs, a selection of materials for the students to build their egg 'crash helmet', for example, egg boxes, plastic bags, straws, newspaper, cotton wool, tissue paper, straw, yogurt pots, tin foil, balloons, sand, sellotape etc., metre ruler.

SAFETY AND TECHNICAL NOTES:
- Ensure that any containers that previously held food have been cleaned.
- Boiling the eggs in advance will prevent any mess caused if the eggs break when dropped.
- Remind the students not to consume the eggs.
- Be aware of any allergies.

Can we make a crash helmet?

METHOD:

To be done in advance by the teacher
Soft-boil the eggs that are to be used in the investigation. You may want to prepare a few more than is required in case there are any breakages whilst the students build their device.

STUDENTS:

1. You have been challenged with designing a model for a new style of crash helmet. Your model crash helmet must be able to protect an egg from a one-metre drop!
2. Spend some time looking at the materials you have been provided. Discuss in your group what designs might work. Sketch the idea for your crash helmet.
3. Build your model crash helmet. You can modify and improve your design as you are building it.
4. When your crash helmet is ready, collect your egg and get ready for the big drop!

DATA COLLECTION IDEAS:
The students can draw or take photographs of their model crash helmets and then take a photograph of their eggs after they have been dropped.

DIFFERENTIATION:
- **Decrease the challenge:** The students can build and test their model crash helmets before coming up with their final design.
- **Increase the challenge:** The students can be given extra criteria to meet, for example a maximum weight for their crash helmet, producing a waterproof crash helmet etc.

USEFUL QUESTIONS TO ASK THE STUDENTS:
1. Which designs/materials were most effective at protecting the egg? Why do you think this was?
2. What other factors would we need to consider if we were designing a crash helmet for someone to wear?
3. Why is it important to wear a crash helmet when performing certain activities, for example riding a bike?

HOMEWORK:
The students can research how crash helmets have been developed and improved.

PROJECT 1

Healthy teeth

LEARNING OBJECTIVES:
Investigate the best ways to keep our teeth healthy.

INTRODUCTION:
The students investigate how to maintain healthy teeth by looking at factors such as diet, toothpaste composition and brushing techniques.

USEFUL PRIOR WORK:
The students should know the basic composition of teeth and their role in digestion.

NATIONAL CURRICULUM LINKS:

Nutrition and digestion
- the content of a healthy human diet: carbohydrates, lipids (fats and oils), proteins, vitamins, minerals, dietary fibre and water, and why each is needed
- the consequences of imbalances in the diet, including obesity, starvation and deficiency diseases
- the tissues and organs of the human digestive system, including adaptations to function and how the digestive system digests food (enzymes simply as biological catalysts).

PROJECT IDEAS:
1 The students can compare the effect different foods have on teeth by using hard-boiled eggs as teeth substitutes. The students can perform a fair-test style investigation by soaking hard-boiled eggs in different liquids, including coke, milk, orange juice, coffee and water, and seeing the effect they have on the eggshell.
2 The students can compare different types of toothpaste including leading brand names, shop's own brand, children's toothpaste and fluoride-free toothpaste. The active ingredients can be compared from the labelling along with other factors such as price, appearance, taste etc. The students can then use the toothpastes to attempt to remove stains from hard-boiled eggshells (the eggs should be soaked in food colouring prior to the investigation).
3 The students can investigate different types of toothbrush and/or brushing techniques. The students can use disclosing tablets in order to show up the plaque present on their own teeth and then brush their teeth with either different toothbrushes or brushing techniques to determine which is the best for removing plaque.
4 The students can compile the information they have gathered on maintaining healthy teeth into a leaflet or PowerPoint aimed at other young people. They can then present their work to the rest of the class.

The investigation for food testing (see Experiment 25) could also be included in this project.

PROJECT 2

Desert island survival

LEARNING OBJECTIVES:

You have been washed up on a desert island! You have to find a way to survive and to signal to passing ships so you can be rescued.

INTRODUCTION:

The students conduct a series of investigations based around survival on a desert island.

USEFUL PRIOR WORK:

The students should be familiar with simple separation techniques and using light and mirrors.

NATIONAL CURRICULUM LINKS:

Pure and impure substances
- the concept of a pure substance
- mixtures, including dissolving
- simple techniques for separating mixtures: filtration, evaporation, distillation and chromatography.

Light
- light waves travelling through a vacuum; speed of light
- the transmission of light through materials: absorption, diffuse scattering and specular reflection at a surface
- use of ray model to explain imaging in mirrors, the pinhole camera, the refraction of light and action of convex lens in focusing (qualitative); the human eye.

Magnetism
- Earth's magnetism, compass and navigation.

PROJECT IDEAS:

The students can perform an investigation each lesson related to the idea of surviving on a desert island. The students could work in small groups and the group that performs the best in the investigations could win 'most likely to survive'.

IDEAS FOR INVESTIGATIONS CAN INCLUDE:

1 Purifying water
The students can be given some dirty water that they need to filter in order to make it clean for drinking. Give the students a selection of different materials such as funnels, cotton wool, sand, charcoal, pebbles (some useful, some not useful) etc., that they can use for filtering water. They can design and test their own system for filtering the water. Discuss with the students that even though the water looks clean it still might not be safe for drinking due to the presence of bacteria. The students could also attempt evaporation and condensation if the water contains salt.

2 Time and place
The students can use magnets in order to make a simple compass from a metal sewing needle. This can be mounted onto a piece of cork and floated in a small dish of water in order to move freely. They can compare this compass to a regular compass in terms of how well it works. The students can also build a simple sundial from paper plates and straws so they are able to tell the time on their island.

3 Keeping healthy

The students can test a selection of food that is found on the island to see which nutrients they contain. They can test for starch, protein and fat and which foods contain vitamin C. They can then design a healthy eating plan for their time on the island.

4 Signal for rescue

The students can use mirrors and some other materials such as cardboard tubes, straws and plastic tubs, to design a 'signalling device' that they can use to attract the attention of passing ships. The students can learn the Morse code signal for SOS and test their devices.

The investigation for building a solar oven (see Experiment 86) could also be included in this project.

PROJECT 3

Environmental survey

LEARNING OBJECTIVES:
You have been tasked with carrying out an environmental survey of the school in order to come up with recommendations on how to improve the school grounds.

INTRODUCTION:
The students conduct a number of environmental surveys of the school grounds.

USEFUL PRIOR WORK:
The students should be familiar with using data-loggers and environmental survey equipment such as pooters.

NATIONAL CURRICULUM LINKS:

Relationships in an ecosystem
- the interdependence of organisms in an ecosystem, including food webs and insect pollinated crops
- the importance of plant reproduction through insect pollination in human food security
- how organisms affect, and are affected by, their environment, including the accumulation of toxic materials.

Inheritance, chromosomes, DNA and genes
- changes in the environment that may leave individuals within a species, and some entire species, less well adapted to compete successfully and reproduce, which in turn may lead to extinction.

PROJECT IDEAS:
The students can perform a different environmental survey each lesson. The students can then use the information to write-up an environmental report of the school including recommendations for how to improve the school environment.

IDEAS FOR INVESTIGATIONS CAN INCLUDE:

1 Mini-beast survey
The students can use pooters, nets and pitfall traps (these can be set up in advance) to conduct a survey on the types of insects that are present on the school grounds. The students can use classification keys in order to identify the organisms. Remind the students to release any insects back where they found them.

2 Plant survey
The students can conduct a survey on the types of plants growing in the school grounds. The students can use classification keys to identify the plants and they can research which insects or birds would be particularly attracted to these plants.

3 Soil analysis
The students can test samples of soil from different parts of the school ground. They can analyse which type of soil it is (sandy, loam, clay), and conduct pH testing and moisture testing (data-loggers could be used for this). The students can then research which plants would grow particularly well in the different soil samples.

4 Report writing

The students can compile their information into an environmental report with recommendations on how to improve the school environment, for example planting certain species of plants or setting up bird feeders. Some of these recommendations could be designed and set up by the students.

The investigation for building a bug hotel (see Experiment 30) could also be included in this project.

PROJECT 4

Set design

LEARNING OBJECTIVES:
You have been tasked with creating a set for the next school play.

INTRODUCTION:
The students create a model set for a school play incorporating lighting and sound effects.

USEFUL PRIOR WORK:
The students should be familiar with using simple electrical circuits, mirrors and light filters.

NATIONAL CURRICULUM LINKS:

Sound waves
- sound needs a medium to travel, the speed of sound in air, in water, in solids
- sound produced by vibrations of objects, in loudspeakers, detected by their effects on microphone diaphragm and the ear drum; sound waves are longitudinal.

Light waves
- the transmission of light through materials: absorption, diffuse scattering and specular reflection at a surface
- use of ray model to explain imaging in mirrors, the pinhole camera, the refraction of light and action of convex lens in focusing (qualitative); the human eye
- colours and the different frequencies of light, white light and prisms (qualitative only); differential colour effects in absorption and diffuse reflection.

Current electricity
- electric current, measured in amperes, in circuits, series and parallel circuits, currents add where branches meet and current as flow of charge.

PROJECT IDEAS:
The students need to plan and build a model set for a school play (real or made-up). The students can be given a list of particular scenes that will need certain effects occurring on the set. The students can build and test their model sets to see how they might work on a larger scale.

IDEAS FOR INVESTIGATIONS CAN INCLUDE:

1 Basic set and lighting
The students can construct a basic square set from cardboard boxes (packaging boxes would be strong enough) including access to the stage from the side of the box and trap doors in the floor. The students can then add a basic lighting system by building an electrical circuit that can be controlled by different switches.

2 Sound design
The students can design a basic sound system for their set by building simple sound speakers from paper plates and using other materials such as balloons as amplifiers.

3 Lighting effects

The students can design additional lighting effects for their set, for example by using coloured filters or translucent and opaque materials. The students can test the effects by shining light from torches that are acting as spotlights.

4 Special effects

The students could design additional special effects for their set, for example using solid carbon dioxide to create dry ice 'smoke', designing a trap door lever system or using vinegar and bicarbonate of soda to create foam.

The investigation for building a dimmer switch (see Experiment 68) could also be included in this project.

PROJECT 5

Olympic science

LEARNING OBJECTIVES:
You have been hired by the British Olympic Team to help improve the performance of their athletes.

INTRODUCTION:
The students investigate the biomechanical and material science factors that influence performance in a particular sport.

USEFUL PRIOR WORK:
The students should be familiar with forces and properties of materials.

NATIONAL CURRICULUM LINKS:

The skeletal and muscular systems
- the structure and functions of the human skeleton, to include support, protection, movement and making blood cells
- biomechanics – the interaction between skeleton and muscles, including the measurement of force exerted by different muscles
- the function of muscles and examples of antagonistic muscles.

Cellular respiration
- aerobic and anaerobic respiration in living organisms, including the breakdown of organic molecules to enable all the other chemical processes necessary for life
- a word summary for aerobic respiration
- the differences between aerobic and anaerobic respiration in terms of the reactants, the products formed and the implications for the organism.

Materials
- properties of ceramics, polymers and composites (qualitative).

Calculation of fuel uses and costs in the domestic context
- comparing energy values of different foods (from labels) (kJ).

Energy changes and transfers
- simple machines give bigger force but at the expense of smaller movement (and vice versa): product of force and displacement unchanged
- other processes that involve energy transfer: changing motion, dropping an object, completing an electrical circuit, stretching a spring, metabolism of food, burning fuels.

Describing motion
- speed and the quantitative relationship between average speed, distance and time (speed = distance ÷ time).

Balanced forces
- opposing forces and equilibrium: weight held by stretched spring or supported on a compressed surface.

Forces and motion
- forces being needed to cause objects to stop or start moving, or to change their speed or direction of motion (qualitative only)
- change depending on direction of force and its size.

PROJECT IDEAS:

The students can be given an Olympic sport (or choose one from a selection – javelin, swimming and long jump are good choices) and carry out research and investigations into how to improve performance in this sport.

IDEAS FOR INVESTIGATIONS CAN INCLUDE:

1 Biomechanics

The students can research the muscles groups, bones and joints that are principally used in their chosen sport. They can investigate the correct physical actions that should be done when carrying out their sport and the effects they have. For example, the students could investigate the best hand position for swimming by using a water trough and dragging their hand through the water.

2 Equipment design

The students can investigate the best materials or design for the equipment needed in their chosen sport. For example, the students could build javelins out of paper in order to investigate the best design.

3 Physics in action

The students could research the forces involved in their chosen sport and can produce force diagrams showing where these forces occur and the effect they will have on athlete performance. The students could also carry out mathematical calculations, for example speed, time and distance calculations for running.

4 Nutrition for sport

The students can research the best diet for an athlete in their chosen sport. They can research if there is any difference between a normal training day diet and the diet on a competition day. The students could investigate energy levels in different foods and plan an appropriate diet.

The investigation on muscle fatigue (see Experiment 12) could also be included in this project.

PROJECT 6

Chocolate lab

LEARNING OBJECTIVES:
You have been asked to design a chocolate bar for a new company.

INTRODUCTION:
The students investigate different properties of chocolate in order to design a new chocolate bar.

USEFUL PRIOR WORK:
The students should be familiar with basic chemical changes.

NATIONAL CURRICULUM LINKS:

The particulate nature of matter
- the properties of the different states of matter (solid, liquid and gas) in terms of the particle model, including gas pressure
- changes of state in terms of the particle model.

Atoms, elements and compounds
- conservation of mass changes of state and chemical reactions.

Pure and impure substances
- the concept of a pure substance
- mixtures, including dissolving.

Nutrition and digestion
- the content of a healthy human diet: carbohydrates, lipids (fats and oils), proteins, vitamins, minerals, dietary fibre and water, and why each is needed
- calculations of energy requirements in a healthy daily diet
- the consequences of imbalances in the diet, including obesity, starvation and deficiency diseases.

PROJECT IDEAS:
The students are challenged to come up with a design for a new chocolate bar. To do this they must first conduct a series of investigations on the properties of chocolate. Access to a food technology lab for this project would be beneficial.

IDEAS FOR INVESTIGATIONS CAN INCLUDE:

1 Melting points
The students can conduct a fair-test style investigation into the melting points of white, milk and dark chocolate. The students could take this further by comparing the melting points of chocolate which have increasing levels of cocoa, i.e. 40%, 50%, 60% etc.

2 Blooming chocolate
The students investigate the causes of bloom (light patches) on chocolate. Blooming can happen when chocolate melts and then re-solidifies. The students can melt chocolate samples and cool them at different rates (room temperature, fridge, freezer etc.) to see the effect this has on blooming.

3 Taste testing
The students can investigate different flavours or foods that can be added to chocolate by conducting taste tests with other students. The students can create some chocolate samples with added flavours and conduct a survey to see which combination is the most popular.

4 Design

The students can create their chocolate bar based on what they have learnt from their research. Tastings can be conducted after the chocolate bars have been made.

The investigation on popping fruit balls (see Experiment 57) could also be included in this project.

PROJECT 7

Scene of crime investigation

LEARNING OBJECTIVES:
Solve the crime that has taken place in the science laboratory.

INTRODUCTION:
The students conduct a series of investigations based on forensic science in order to solve a crime that has taken place.

USEFUL PRIOR WORK:
The students should be familiar with forces and with using microscopes.

NATIONAL CURRICULUM LINKS:

Cells and organisation
- cells as the fundamental unit of living organisms, including how to observe, interpret and record cell structure using a light microscope.

Inheritance, chromosomes, DNA and genes
- heredity as the process by which genetic information is transmitted from one generation to the next
- the variation between individuals within a species being continuous or discontinuous, to include measurement and graphical representation of variation.

Pure and impure substances
- the concept of a pure substance
- simple techniques for separating mixtures: filtration, evaporation, distillation and chromatography.

Describing motion
- speed and the quantitative relationship between average speed, distance and time (speed = distance ÷ time).

Forces
- non-contact forces: gravity forces acting at a distance on Earth and in space, forces between magnets, and forces due to static electricity.

Forces and motion
- forces being needed to cause objects to stop or start moving, or to change their speed or direction of motion (qualitative only)
- change depending on direction of force and its size.

PROJECT IDEAS:
The students are challenged to solve a fictional crime that has taken place in the science laboratory. To do this the students conduct a series of mini-investigations and then compile the information together. It is necessary to have five suspects for this investigation and to ensure that the results will eventually allow the students to identify the suspect when they have all been gathered.

IDEAS FOR INVESTIGATIONS CAN INCLUDE:

1 Hair analysis
A hair from the suspect can be found at the crime scene. The students can examine the hair under the microscope along with hair from the suspects in order to identify what colour hair the suspect had. This investigation could eliminate one suspect.

2 Fibre analysis
A fibre from the suspect's clothing can be found at the crime scene. The students can examine the fibre under the microscope and observe how it burns in order to identify what type of fibre it is. This investigation could eliminate one suspect.

3 Footprint analysis
A partial footprint from the suspect can be found at the crime scene. The students can make a plaster cast of the print and examine the resulting cast and try to match it to photographs of the suspect's shoes. This investigation could eliminate one suspect.

4 Chromatography
A note written by the suspect can be found at the crime scene. The students can perform chromatography on the note and compare the results with chromatography carried out on pens belonging to the suspect.

The investigation on blood spatter (see Experiment 72) could also be included in this project.

PROJECT 8

Fairground games

LEARNING OBJECTIVES:
Design and build a game for a fairground.

INTRODUCTION:
The students design and build a fairground style game using at least one scientific principle.

USEFUL PRIOR WORK:
The students should be familiar with forces and electricity.

NATIONAL CURRICULUM LINKS:

Forces
- forces as pushes or pulls, arising from the interaction between two objects
- using force arrows in diagrams, adding forces in one dimension, balanced and unbalanced forces
- moment as the turning effect of a force
- forces: associated with deforming objects; stretching and squashing – springs; with rubbing and friction between surfaces, with pushing things out of the way; resistance to motion of air and water.

Pressure in fluids
- pressure in liquids, increasing with depth; upthrust effects, floating and sinking.

Forces and motion
- forces being needed to cause objects to stop or start moving, or to change their speed or direction of motion (qualitative only).

Current electricity
- electric current, measured in amperes, in circuits, series and parallel circuits, currents add where branches meet and current as flow of charge
- potential difference, measured in volts, battery and bulb ratings; resistance, measured in ohms, as the ratio of potential difference (p.d.) to current.

PROJECT IDEAS:
The students are challenged to design and build a model of a game that would be suitable for a fairground. The amount of guidance provided for this investigation can vary; it could be left completely open-ended or the students can be given a more focused challenge. Ideas for games could include electric circuit style games such as steady-hand games or electronic quizzes, forces-based games such as 'test of strength', light-based games such as hall of mirrors, or any other game that makes use of a scientific principle.

IDEAS FOR INVESTIGATIONS CAN INCLUDE:

1 Brainstorming
The students can brainstorm initial ideas for their game. Provide them with photos of different types of fairground games to provide some inspiration. Show them the type of equipment they will be able to use when making their game. Encourage them to have decided on what type of game they will be making by the end of the lesson.

2 Design

The students can plan the design for their fairground game including identifying what materials they will need. The students should produce a detailed, annotated diagram for their game by the end of the lesson.

3 Build

The students can build their fairground game and make any necessary modifications as they build the game. Encourage them to test the game as they go along to ensure everything works as planned. The students may need two lessons to complete their builds depending on how complex their games are.

4 Test

The students can test and then present their games to the rest of the class. The students can test each other's games and then evaluate their own design.

PROJECT 9

Aeroplane design

LEARNING OBJECTIVES:
Design and make the best model aeroplane.

INTRODUCTION:
The students design and make a model aeroplane that will travel the furthest in a race.

USEFUL PRIOR WORK:
The students should be familiar with forces.

NATIONAL CURRICULUM LINKS:

Forces
- forces as pushes or pulls, arising from the interaction between two objects
- using force arrows in diagrams, adding forces in one dimension, balanced and unbalanced forces
- moment as the turning effect of a force
- forces: associated with deforming objects; stretching and squashing – springs; with rubbing and friction between surfaces, with pushing things out of the way; resistance to motion of air and water.

Describing motion
- speed and the quantitative relationship between average speed, distance and time (speed = distance ÷ time).

PROJECT IDEAS:
The students are challenged to design and make a model aeroplane that will travel the furthest in a race. The students can investigate various factors that will affect the performance of their aeroplane before competing with the rest of the students.

IDEAS FOR INVESTIGATIONS CAN INCLUDE:

1 Shape
The students can research the different shapes that are found in aeroplane design and incorporate this into their designs. The students can produce sketches for the overall design of their aeroplane.

2 Materials
The students can be supplied with a selection of different materials from which they can build their aeroplanes, for example different types of paper, card, acetate etc. The students could make different versions of their planes and test which materials work the best.

3 Thrust and drag
The students can investigate the best way to launch their aeroplanes in order to obtain the best flight path. They could also look at whether they should add any extra weight or drag to their planes to improve the flight direction. This will be particularly important if the race is taking place outside.

4 Test
The students can compete in a competition to see which plane is able to travel the furthest or straightest or through certain obstacles, for example a plastic hoop. The students can evaluate their designs after the competition and suggest what improvements they might make.

PROJECT 10

What's the weather like?

LEARNING OBJECTIVES:
Conduct a weather survey for our school and produce a weather impact report.

INTRODUCTION:
The students carry out a weather survey by investigating various aspects of weather within the school grounds.

USEFUL PRIOR WORK:
The students should be familiar with ecology and photosynthesis.

NATIONAL CURRICULUM LINKS:

Photosynthesis
- the reactants in, and products of, photosynthesis, and a word summary for photosynthesis
- the dependence of almost all life on Earth on the ability of photosynthetic organisms, such as plants and algae, to use sunlight in photosynthesis to build organic molecules that are an essential energy store and to maintain levels of oxygen and carbon dioxide in the atmosphere.

Relationships in an ecosystem
- how organisms affect, and are affected by, their environment, including the accumulation of toxic materials.

Chemical reactions
- the pH scale for measuring acidity/alkalinity; and indicators.

Earth and atmosphere
- the composition of the atmosphere
- the production of carbon dioxide by human activity and the impact on climate.

PROJECT IDEAS:
The students carry out a detailed weather survey based in the school grounds. This project can be carried out at any time of the year but the factors the students investigate may have to be modified to fit in with the seasons.

IDEAS FOR INVESTIGATIONS CAN INCLUDE:

1 Rain and wind
The students can design and build a rain collector (in order to test the acidity of the collected rain) and an anemometer (in order to measure wind speed). The rain collectors can be set up in suitable locations and the students can use the anemometer to measure the wind speed in different locations around the school.

2 Light and heat
The students can use data-loggers with light sensors in order to measure light levels in different locations around the school. They can also take temperature readings for the ambient temperature and the temperature of the soil and any water features such as ponds.

3 Rain water

The students can measure how much rain has been collected in their rain collectors and also test the acidity levels of the rain. The acidity levels of any water features in the school, such as ponds, can also be measured.

4 Weather impact report

The students can compile the information they have collected into a weather impact report, which can be presented to the rest of the class or school. The students can evaluate what impact the weather will have on the local wildlife and plants of the school.

Index

Acids and alkalis 81, 94, 96, 115, 121, 123

Bacteria 2, 38
Biomechanics 24, 34, 194

Cells 4, 40, 198
Chemical changes 71, 102, 110, 115
Combustion 71
Crystals 119

Decomposition 12, 14
Diffusion 22
Dissolving 113
DNA 4, 30, 46, 54, 56, 198

Electricity 90, 133, 139, 145, 165, 179, 200
Energy 20, 71, 163, 167, 173, 175, 183, 189, 192
Enzymes 18, 24, 77

Fermentation 60
Food and digestion 8, 14, 20, 44, 50, 52, 117, 187
Forces 141, 143, 147, 151, 153, 185, 194, 200, 202

Heart 36, 63

Identifying substance 106, 108, 189
Insects 32, 61, 190

Light 127, 157, 159, 177, 189, 192
Lungs 6, 63

Magnetism 155, 189
Metals 73, 79, 96
Microscopes 2, 40

Particle theory 65, 75, 92, 117, 135, 169, 171, 196
Periodic table 98, 100
Physical changes 84, 88, 102, 137, 171
Plants 10, 16, 26, 28, 42, 48, 94, 104, 203
Polymers 106, 125
Pressure 129, 200

Radiation 167
Rates of reactions 86
Rusting 79
Rocks and soil 67, 104, 119, 121

Separating 69, 198
Space 141
Surveys 28, 30, 48, 190

Waves 131, 149, 161

Taylor & Francis eBooks

Helping you to choose the right eBooks for your Library

Add Routledge titles to your library's digital collection today. Taylor and Francis ebooks contains over 50,000 titles in the Humanities, Social Sciences, Behavioural Sciences, Built Environment and Law.

Choose from a range of subject packages or create your own!

Benefits for you
- Free MARC records
- COUNTER-compliant usage statistics
- Flexible purchase and pricing options
- All titles DRM-free.

REQUEST YOUR FREE INSTITUTIONAL TRIAL TODAY

Free Trials Available
We offer free trials to qualifying academic, corporate and government customers.

Benefits for your user
- Off-site, anytime access via Athens or referring URL
- Print or copy pages or chapters
- Full content search
- Bookmark, highlight and annotate text
- Access to thousands of pages of quality research at the click of a button.

eCollections – Choose from over 30 subject eCollections, including:

Archaeology	Language Learning
Architecture	Law
Asian Studies	Literature
Business & Management	Media & Communication
Classical Studies	Middle East Studies
Construction	Music
Creative & Media Arts	Philosophy
Criminology & Criminal Justice	Planning
Economics	Politics
Education	Psychology & Mental Health
Energy	Religion
Engineering	Security
English Language & Linguistics	Social Work
Environment & Sustainability	Sociology
Geography	Sport
Health Studies	Theatre & Performance
History	Tourism, Hospitality & Events

For more information, pricing enquiries or to order a free trial, please contact your local sales team: **www.tandfebooks.com/page/sales**

Routledge — Taylor & Francis Group | The home of Routledge books | **www.tandfebooks.com**